Also by the Author

BPMN Method and Style (2nd edition 2011)

BPMN Quick and Easy (2017)

DMN Cookbook (2018)

DMN Method and Style (2nd edition 2018)

CMMN METHOD AND STYLE

Bruce Silver

CODY-CASSIDY PRESS

CMMN Method and Style

By Bruce Silver
ISBN 978-0-9823681-9-0

Published by Cody-Cassidy Press, Altadena, CA 91001 USA
Contact
info@cody-cassidy.com
+1 (831) 331-6341

TABLE OF CONTENTS

Preface

Those familiar with my past writings may be surprised that I have written a book on the Case Management Model and Notation (CMMN) standard, because when CMMN was launched in 2014, I was unenthusiastic and vocal about it. Business process modeling already had a standard – BPMN 2.0 – that was widely adopted by both business and technical modelers. Why did we now need a different one? CMMN's creators maintained that it was necessary because there are many kinds of processes that BPMN is unable to handle. Although BPMN could have been tweaked to handle them, those tweaks never happened. In my opinion, they never will; the BPMN 2.0 spec appears to be forever frozen in stone.

Actually, CMMN's backers have a valid point. BPMN does have limitations, and in my BPMN Method and Style training we discuss them. Those limitations mostly stem from the fact that BPMN's conception of a *process* is quite narrow, much narrower in fact than that of BPM Architecture and most other areas of business process management. For example, many of the "processes" listed in APQC's Process Classification Framework are not what BPMN would call processes, and many cannot be modeled in BPMN at all. CMMN, on the other hand, could handle them. That's reason number one for my change of heart. Instead of describing the logic procedurally – following a defined sequence of steps – CMMN logic is *declarative*, each case element independently defining its own prerequisite conditions. That gives it great flexibility, but makes the logic harder to communicate clearly.

A second reason was the observation that leading innovators in business process technology are now beginning to adopt and promote CMMN. For example, Trisotech's Digital Automation Suite uses CMMN in conjunction with BPMN and DMN to create a business-friendly model-driven platform based entirely on industry standards. Also, at the annual bpmNEXT conference[1] that I host together with Nathanial Palmer of BPM.com, Flowable's CMMN-based demos[2] have walked off with the Best in Show award two years in a row. And in the past year,

---

[1] www.bpmnext.com

[2] https://documents.bpm.com/bpmnext/bpmnext2019/presentations/bpmnext2019-flowable.pdf

FICO, a leading decision management vendor, has made CMMN a key part of its solution development methodology, called xDRAW.[3]

After years of relative obscurity, CMMN is finally attracting the attention of leading technology innovators, completing the triad of business modeling and automation standards from the Object Management Group (OMG) – BPMN (process modeling), DMN (decision modeling), and CMMN (case modeling). Trisotech, Flowable, and FICO are all basing their business automation projects on that triad.

Method and Style

Once I accepted CMMN's rationale, I could see that it was badly in need of a book. You cannot learn a modeling language from the spec, which is written for tool vendors, and a quick check of Amazon.com revealed zero CMMN books in print. Moreover, CMMN was in need of *Method and Style* as well, an approach I developed over a decade ago for BPMN and have since applied to DMN. Whereas the requirements specified in OMG's business modeling standards emphasize precise execution semantics, modelers need something more: the ability to communicate the underlying logic to all stakeholders from the diagrams alone, without defining execution-related details usually left to programmers. That's what Method and Style tries to provide.

Method and Style is a set of modeling conventions layered on top of the official rules of the standard. Created for non-executable models defined by business users, Method and Style encourages models that communicate the logic clearly and completely through the printed diagrams alone. Although all three of OMG's business automation standards in theory claim two objectives – *visual communication of the model logic* through diagrams and tables, and *direct execution of the model logic* on an automation engine – the rules of the specs, in reality, concern only the latter.

Having delivered BPMN training since 2007, I know that just a tiny fraction of BPMN models are intended for execution. Instead they are used for process documentation, analysis, and improvement. For those users the only thing that counts is what is displayed in the diagrams. From the perspective of the spec, defining the process logic precisely requires adding variables and executable gateway expressions, details normally delegated to programmers and which do not appear in the diagrams. That often leaves the process logic ambiguous and incomplete to stakeholders without direct access to the modeling tool.

BPMN Method and Style

Method and Style takes the view that any model details important to understanding the logic must be expressed somehow in the diagrams. Thus BPMN Method and Style imposes various conventions that *imply* the existence of certain variables and gateway expressions simply from the *labels* of end events and gates. Those conventions make the process logic clear from the

---

[3] https://slideplayer.com/slide/14292614/

diagrams alone, with requiring modelers to actually define variables and executable expressions. In addition, various icons, symbols, and labels called optional in the spec are *required* by Method and Style. Method and Style's conventions can be formalized as *style rules* – in addition to the rules of the spec – that can be applied as validation checks on the models.

CMMN Method and Style

With CMMN, the situation is similar. Making the case logic complete and unambiguous requires definition of variables and executable expressions for the entry and exit conditions of case model elements (called *plan items*), details that normally are not displayed in the diagrams. CMMN Method and Style applies conventions that *imply* the existence of certain variables and condition expressions based on *labels* of diagram elements, such as milestones and sentries. With these conventions, a wide variety of case behaviors can be described unambiguously from the printed diagrams alone.

Since CMMN's declarative logic paradigm is unfamiliar to most users, diagrams are prone to modeling errors, such as tasks that repeat forever with no way to stop except manual termination, or deadlocked stages, unable to complete. Many such errors can be detected by the style rules as well.

Some tools, like those of Trisotech, provide automated *model validation* based on the style rules. When Method and Style's rules are enforced by model validation, my own experience of BPMN and DMN training has shown them to greatly improve model quality and clarity. Thus, in addition to explaining CMMN from the perspective of the spec, this book explains the Method and Style conventions, including the style rules.

Writing the book also revealed occasional inconsistencies and ambiguities in the CMMN spec itself, motivating a series of discussions with both Trisotech and Flowable about what the spec actually intends and how to handle the problem areas. CMMN Method and Style reflects the consensus of those discussions.

Structure of the Book

The book explains the concepts of CMMN, its basic elements, and usage of these elements in various styles of case management models. In addition, it explains the Method and Style conventions, the reasons for them, and their representation in the diagrams.

I recommend that readers go through the chapters in order, although Chapter 8, *Declarative Modeling Patterns*, may serve as a helpful reference for certain behaviors shown in earlier chapters, as well as those the modeler may encounter in practice.

Chapter 1, *What Is CMMN?*, shows how case management fits in the business process management landscape. We describe how cases differ from the "structured" processes of BPMN and provide examples of typical case management scenarios. We then discuss how the CMMN standard came about, in many respects as a reaction to BPMN.

Chapter 2, *Case Plan Elements*, explains the building blocks of a CMMN diagram, or *Case Plan Model*. The case diagram shows the various actions that could take place in each state of the case, as well as how completion of those actions, in combination with other events, drive overall case behavior. We discuss the various types of *tasks*, the actions of a case, and *stages*, containers of the case plan elements available in a particular state of the case. In this chapter we also explain CMMN's declarative logic paradigm, based on the *lifecycle state* of tasks, stages, and other model elements, as well as CMMN's *event-condition-action* mechanism.

Chapter 3, *Case File Model*, discusses case data elements, known collectively as *case file items*. Not all case file items are visualized in the diagrams, but file item *standard events* – such as *create*, *update*, or *delete* – are displayed in the diagram if they trigger advancement of the case plan. We also introduce the Method and Style concept of *implicit file items* that capture the state of a task or milestone for use in condition expressions in event-condition-action logic.

Chapter 4, *Modeling Case Logic*, shows how the various diagram elements are used in combination to describe activity flow in a declarative manner. We discuss the conditions under which a CMMN task or stage starts and completes and the benefits of using BPMN and CMMN in combination. We extend BPMN Method and Style's concept of *end states* to tasks and stages in CMMN, including their visual representation in the diagrams.

Chapter 5, *Styles of Case Modeling*, illustrates three basic styles used in CMMN models: user-driven, event-condition-action (ECA), and hierarchical. Typically, a CMMN model contains a mix of all three styles. In the user-driven style, the case advances based on manual user action, selecting from a menu of available actions such as completing or terminating a task or stage, or starting an available task or stage. In the ECA style, the case advances automatically based on declarative logic defined at design time, in which lifecycle *events* of plan items and file items, in combination with file item *conditions*, determine whether a task or stage starts, completes, or exits. In the hierarchical style, stages typically represent exclusive states of the case. The top-level diagram displays stages in collapsed form and shows the logic determining which stage is active at any time. The details of each stage are shown in hyperlinked child-level diagrams.

Chapter 6, *CMMN by Example: Social Care*, presents a detailed real-world example based on social care in a European country, using elements of all three case modeling styles.

Chapter 7, *Style Rules*, explains the Method and Style model validation rules. The style rules are not part of the CMMN spec. They are just my own recommendations, intended to (1) make the case logic clear from the printed diagrams, and (2) warn against logic that could lead to unintended behavior, such as deadlocked models.

Chapter 8, *Declarative Modeling Patterns*, explains CMMN's various ECA "micropatterns" with reference to equivalent BPMN patterns using Method and Style. This chapter can be used as a reference for understanding other models in the book as well as real scenarios encountered by the modeler. Readers familiar with BPMN may want to read this chapter before Chapter 6.

Chapter 9, *Executable CMMN with Method and Style*, explains how executable CMMN tools can integrate Method and Style by automatically generating variables and condition expressions implied by the labels of various diagram elements.

Acknowledgments

This book would not have been possible without the efforts of Trisotech to create a tool that is not only faithful to the CMMN standard but adds support for the Method and Style conventions, including automated style rule validation. Trisotech Case Modeler was used to create the diagrams used in the book, and I urge readers to go to www.trisotech.com to request a free trial of the software.

Special thanks go to Denis Gagne, Simon Ringuette, and Maciej Swiderski, the brains behind Trisotech Case Modeler, who also provided extensive review and comments on the book drafts. I could not have wished for better partners. I also received generous review and comments from members of Flowable's CMMN team, including Paul Holmes-Higgin, Joram Barrez, Micha Kiener, and Tijs Rademakers. Thank you all so much!

I am grateful as well to Serge Schiltz of processCentric GmbH, who contributed the Social Care scenario described in Chapter 6. I took some liberties with it, so don't blame Serge for any discrepancy between that model and "the way it ought to work."

Thanks also to Carol Leyba for cover design and other assistance, as always.

Bruce Silver
Pasadena, CA, May 2020

CHAPTER 1

What Is CMMN?

What Is Case Management?

The term *case management* has a long history in the domains of healthcare and social services. If you Google the term, it is most often described as a client care "process" that progresses through stages of Screening, Assessing, Stratifying Risk, Planning, Implementing (Care Coordination), Following-Up, Transitioning (Transitional Care), Communicating Post Transition, and Evaluating Results. But that is NOT what this book is about. In the context of this book, case management is a style of business process management (BPM) applicable generally to office work – not just in healthcare and social services – in which the "process" is not well described by the standard language of BPM, called BPMN.

The essential distinguishing characteristic of case management is the "unstructured" nature of its activity flow logic. In BPMN, a process instance progresses through a sequence of steps described explicitly as paths in a diagram leading from a single start event to one or more end events. For any particular instance of the process, the path followed might be determined by human judgment, external events, and business rules, but the steps, branching logic, and exception paths are all defined in advance and shown in the process diagram.

In case management, by contrast, the logic often cannot be expressed as task sequences defined explicitly in advance. In case management, human judgment, events, and data conditions don't determine paths through a predefined diagram. Instead, those things determine which activities – out of a menu of possibilities – are *available* to be performed at any time. While this flexibility is an essential ingredient of many types of real-world processes, those processes are not easily modeled in BPMN, which requires all possible activity paths to be completely defined in advance.

In case management, the activities *allowed* to be performed at any time, or *required* in order to complete some phase of the case, are determined by a combination of human judgment, events occurring at runtime, and conditions on case data. Also, a case may span multiple processes, each of which is possibly well-described by BPMN, but where behavior of the case as a whole cannot be modeled in BPMN.

Despite these differences, case management suffers from the same problems as conventional structured process management. Cases take too long to complete. Resources are not used efficiently. Information is misplaced or not retained. There is little or no standardization across the organization. It is difficult to enforce compliance with policies, regulations, and best practices. Visibility is lacking into key performance indicators, either at the individual case level in real time or historical trends in the aggregate. BPMN-based software brings relief for all of these issues with structured processes. Case management needs similar capabilities, but this requires a different type of software based on a different modeling language: CMMN.

Applications of Case Management

Case management scenarios are a common occurrence in many industry segments, including government, insurance, banking and credit, legal, and healthcare.

Dispute Resolution

A good example of dispute resolution concerns billing and credit card disputes. Processing payments is a conventional structured process, but when a customer disputes a charge or demands a refund, case management is usually required.

Even if the credit card issuer provides a standard form for initiating the case, the activities required to resolve each case depend on a myriad of factors. What is the reason for the dispute? Were the goods delivered or services provided? Were they defective? Was the defect the fault of the manufacturer, the shipper, the customer, or some other party? Does the dispute concern the amount of the charge? And so forth.

Resolution of the dispute could depend on any or all of these factors, each of which typically involves production and review of documents. The credit card company may require information from the customer; the manufacturer, retailer, or service provider; the shipper; possibly legal counsel, attorneys, or even law enforcement. The rules involved could depend on the customer's location. As the facts unfold, new tasks and documents may be added to the case.

In the end, there is no way to define in advance the credit card company's dispute resolution "process" as an explicit flow from case initiation to resolution. But many of the same factors that motivate conventional BPM – timely resolution, efficient utilization of resources, compliance, and end-to-end performance visibility – are still important.

Other examples of dispute resolution case management include healthcare claims and grievance procedures, HR termination, and civil litigation and mediation.

Benefits Administration

Case management is well established in many segments of benefits administration, particularly in the public sector. Examples include disability, veterans' benefits, welfare assistance, student financial aid, and grants programs. Within a single case there are issues of eligibility, disbursement of funds or services, changing circumstances of the beneficiary, reporting and compliance.

Underwriting

In various segments of financial services, including commercial lending, life and disability insurance, and securities, the underwriting process is really case management. The activities and documents required depend on the circumstances of each case. While the components of "standard" cases may be predictable, there are many exceptions, requiring additional input from lawyers, accountants, regulators, and investigators.

Project Management

An application area that could benefit from case management BPM, but has received little attention to date, falls under the heading of project management. Examples include launch of a new product or service, a major IT system upgrade, or mergers and acquisitions. There may be relatively few instances of a particular type of case, but each may represent high value and high risk. As with the other examples, the significant attribute is the fact that unanticipated tasks and processes may be added once the project is underway. Project management software typically provides just planning and tracking; case management adds the dimensions of task automation, enforcement of business rules, and application integration.

Evolution of Case Management

Early Efforts

Software to model, automate, and track such unstructured processes long predates CMMN. In fact, it even predates BPMN 1.0, which was developed around 2002. My first encounter with it was in the late 1990s in a product called Workfolder, created by Mordechai Beizer of Eastman Software. I was an independent industry analyst at that time, having previously been the principal analyst for document management and workflow at BIS Strategic Decisions, which became Giga and was later acquired by Forrester Research. I mention my own background because I knew about all the process management products – called "workflow" back then – in the market at that time and I had never seen anything like this.

Instead of routing information from task to task, Workfolder simply maintained a folder of all the information collected or developed in the course of an extended business process – a case – along with task assignments and placeholders for documents required for case completion. That folder was shared by all case workers. In addition to required tasks and placeholders defined at design time, case workers could add new ones freely at runtime. In those days before web services, case information was primarily in the form of documents and marking a task completed was something done manually by a case worker.

Workfolder was hosted on Microsoft Outlook, in hindsight an unfortunate choice, but a decade later it was rewritten as Case 360 from Global 360, now part of Open Text. Workfolder/Case 360 embodied many of the key attributes of CMMN today that distinguish it from BPMN:

- Information primarily in the form of documents not data
- A case folder containing all information, tasks, and case history, shared by case workers
- Order of task performance determined by a combination of user action at runtime and events, not a predefined workflow model

The Rise of BPM Standards

Before the internet era, all software to manage business processes of any type, including case management, was proprietary. There simply were no vendor-independent standards. That all changed with the web.

BPMN was the first vendor-independent standard in the business process domain. It was created around 2002 to automate processes composed of activities implemented as web services. BPMN defined the process logic using diagrams based on the notation of swimlane flowcharts, which were already familiar to business users and widely used in the process improvement community. As a result, BPMN was easily accepted by business users, even though few had any interest in automating their processes. It turned out that BPMN's original process automation language conflicted with still-evolving web service standards, causing it to be replaced with a different execution language called BPEL, even though BPEL didn't exactly fit with the BPMN notation.

Fast forward to 2008, the heyday of Service Oriented Architecture (SOA), an IT initiative that sought to break up monolithic enterprise applications into collections of services that could be sequentially invoked through APIs. To make SOA more appealing to business, major software vendors like IBM, Oracle, and SAP needed a better way than BPEL to connect it with BPMN, which business users liked. The result was BPMN 2.0, which preserved the business-friendly look and feel of swimlane diagrams but added precise execution semantics that allowed BPMN models to be executed on an automation engine.

That strategy worked extremely well for a wide spectrum of business processes, but not all of them. And even though BPMN diagrams were – and still are today – mostly used for process documentation and analysis not automation, their semantics are based on the paradigm of automated service orchestration. BPMN, however, is not well suited to scenarios where the order of activities cannot be prescribed in advance, where some activities are optional, and where what happens next depends largely on the judgment of knowledge workers informed by documents rather than data.

BPMN's Conception of a Process

In BPMN, a *process* is a sequence of activities performed *repeatedly* in the course of business. They don't all have to follow the same path, but each repetition or *instance* of the process must follow some path described in the BPMN diagram, leading from a single *start event* to some end event in the diagram. In Method and Style, each process end event represents a distinct *end state* of the process, describing *how* did that process instance end, successfully or in some exception state.

In a BPMN process, all possible sequences of activities in the process must be defined in advance, as well as the logic that determines which way to go at each branch point in the flow, even those where the logic is simply human choice. A process is like a train going down a track. It can only follow tracks defined in the diagram; it cannot magically jump, as circumstances might require, to some other activity, or skip the next activity on the track.

BPMN models describe processes performed repeatedly, each repletion constituting an *instance* of the process. The notion of process instance is central to BPMN. Each instance has a definite start and must end in one of the defined end states. Although it is not well understood by many BPMN users, the instance of each activity in a BPMN process must have one-to-one correspondence with the instance of the process itself. Thus, if the process instance represents an order to be fulfilled, every activity in the process must pertain to that one order. A weekly update of the item prices, for example, cannot be part of the order process. It must be part of a separate process that runs weekly.

These constraints on a process, essential to the efficiency of a high-performance process automation engine, set BPMN apart from other parts of the BPM world, which use the term process more loosely.

In BPM Architecture frameworks like APQC, for example, most of the Level 3 elements, which they term *Processes*, do not meet BPMN's definition. Many are so-called *management processes*, with names using verbs like "Manage", "Monitor", or "Maintain". They are not performed repeatedly on instances, each with a definite start and end, but rather are performed *continuously*. In others, the exact activity sequence or flow logic cannot be defined in advance, but depends instead on the initiative of knowledge workers, who presumably know what to do when in order to move the process along.

CMMN as a Reaction to BPMN

CMMN arose out of the need to provide modeling and execution of processes like these, left behind by BPMN. Where BPMN seemingly wanted to turn all task performers into robots, CMMN instead would put knowledge workers in charge. What actions occur when would be determined primarily by human judgment, not explicit logic recorded in the model. Moreover, this judgment would be informed primarily by *documents*, not processable data.

In fact, the whole notion of *procedural modeling* of a process – after this do that – would be replaced by *declarative modeling*: Each case task would independently define its own start and completion conditions. It would be enabled to start – or in some cases start automatically – whenever its start conditions were satisfied, which in many cases were simply when its phase or *stage* of the case was active. And it would be available to complete, or possibly autocomplete, when its completion conditions were satisfied. There would be no constraints like alignment of the task and process instance, or even well-defined end states, to worry about. It would be much more flexible than BPMN, able to handle a wider range of business processes.

Of course, if all case logic is based on ad-hoc judgment of knowledge workers, it is not very interesting as a modeling language. It's basically just a list of possible actions at each stage of the case. So, to make it a language worth standardizing, CMMN would also include an *event-condition-action* paradigm, providing tasks and stages also with automated rule-based entry and exit conditions. The case model would be able to indicate, for example, that WHEN a certain event occurs, and IF a certain data condition is true, a task or stage becomes enabled to start or in some cases starts automatically. CMMN would provide a set of *standard events* for its model elements, such as the start or completion of a task, creation or update of a case file item, or achievement of a milestone. In this way, CMMN would be capable of describing behavior ranging from logic-free cases advanced manually by knowledge workers to fully automated sequences triggered by events.

The Drive for an Alternative Standard

In 2009, the need for such an alternative standard began to be formalized at the Object Management Group (OMG), the body behind BPMN. Cordys, one of the principal authors of CMMN, summarized the following "Case management modeling essentials":

- Case management is about higher-level coordination, which cannot simply be tracked by a single process instance.

- It focuses on guiding decisions, in order to reach the goal of the case effectively and efficiently.

- Modeling of case management is not concerned with laying out sequences of activities. It is rather concerned with constraining the choices that can be made with respect to the work to be done, and with respect to how the case evolves.

An RFP for CMMN was issued in May 2009. The CMMN 1.0 standard was released in May 2014 and was updated to version 1.1 in 2016.

> The initiative has been born from a need. In practice it appeared to be difficult to manage case management processes based on BPMN. Proprietary approaches appeared to be more successful. But the industry is served best by standardized approaches, and hence an additional OMG standard would be very helpful.

> The RFP aims for a different paradigm for process control than BPMN currently supports or will support with BPMN 2.0, although it should be possible to smoothly integrate case management models and BPMN process models. Case management is about higher-level coordination, which cannot simply be tracked by a single process instance (like an instance of a BPMN process). It focuses on guiding decisions, in order to reach the goal of the case effectively and efficiently. Modeling of case management is not concerned with laying out sequences of activities (like in BPMN). It is rather concerned with constraining the choices that can be made with respect to the work to be done, and with respect to how the case evolves.

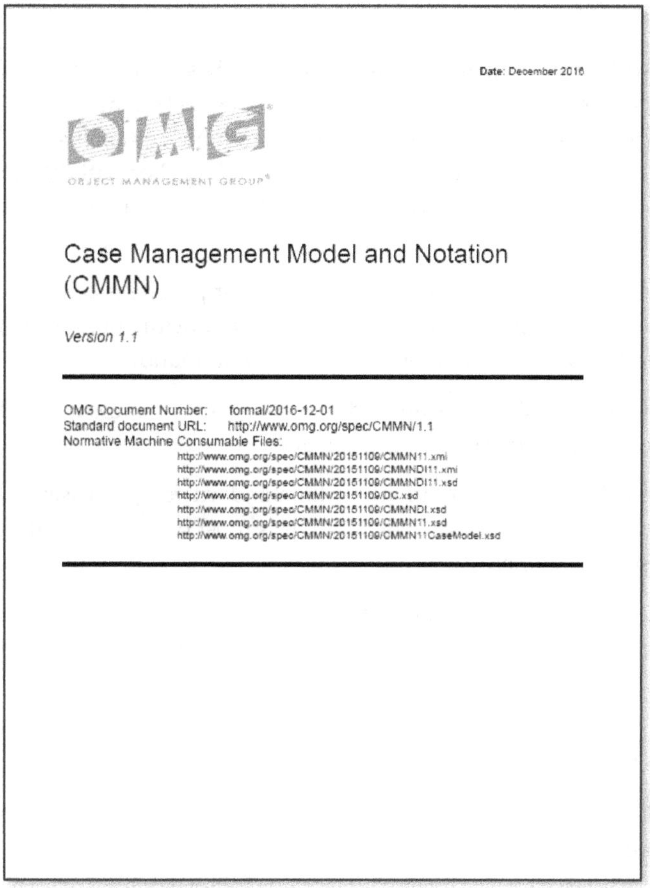

Date: December 2016

OMG

OBJECT MANAGEMENT GROUP®

Case Management Model and Notation (CMMN)

Version 1.1

OMG Document Number: formal/2016-12-01
Standard document URL: http://www.omg.org/spec/CMMN/1.1
Normative Machine Consumable Files:
       http://www.omg.org/spec/CMMN/20151109/CMMN11.xmi
       http://www.omg.org/spec/CMMN/20151109/CMMNDI11.xmi
       http://www.omg.org/spec/CMMN/20151109/CMMNDI11.xsd
       http://www.omg.org/spec/CMMN/20151109/DC.xsd
       http://www.omg.org/spec/CMMN/20151109/CMMNDI.xsd
       http://www.omg.org/spec/CMMN/20151109/CMMN11.xsd
       http://www.omg.org/spec/CMMN/20151109/CMMN11CaseModel.xsd

Figure 1. CMMN is an industry standard

In summary, then, case management describes business processes where the activity flow…

- …is not strictly defined and repeatable
- …depends on evolving circumstances and events
- …depends on ad hoc decisions by knowledge workers
- …depends on details of the particular context (a case)

To accommodate that, CMMN requires…

- …flexibility due to the dynamic nature of the work
- …adaptability to the current informational context
- …knowledge worker control over what to do next (best next action)
- …collaboration with external stakeholders and information sources

CMMN Overview

Like BPMN, CMMN is a business-oriented modeling language. It describes through *diagrams* the behavior of a case – its progression through various *stages* and the *tasks* that could be performed in each stage – for purposes ranging from documentation to analysis for improvement to automation on a case management software platform. Together with BPMN and DMN, CMMN completes the triad of core business automation modeling standards from the Object Management Group (OMG):

- BPMN (Business Process Model and Notation) is the standard for processes described as sequential activity flows. It is primarily used for process documentation and analysis, although occasionally used for model-based process automation.

- DMN (Decision Model and Notation) is the standard for describing business decision logic. It is used both to document and execute business decision logic.

- CMMN (Case Management Model and Notation) is the standard for processes not easily described as sequential activity flows. Like DMN, it is most often used both to document and execute case management.

While each standard is often used standalone, in most case management scenarios it is best to use them together, each language handling the piece it does best, and that is the approach taken in this book.

Like its sister standards, CMMN provides a well-defined diagramming notation based on a formal UML metamodel and XML interchange format. It precisely defines the model's execution semantics, focused on the processes left behind by BPMN, characterized as:

- Knowledge worker focused
- Document-centric
- Declarative
- Event-driven
- "Unpredictable"

Model-Based

CMMN is *model-based*. The case logic is defined by diagrams and the properties of diagram elements, not by program code. To make the logic executable, there may be code, of course, to implement the case tasks (actions) and user interfaces, but the *case logic* that specifies which actions can occur at any stage of the case is determined entirely by the model.

Model elements include case plan items, case file items, and case roles.

- The activity flow logic, or *case plan*, is defined in diagrams using defined shapes and symbols representing distinct types of *plan items*.

- Case data, called the *case file*, is a collection of *file items* comprised of folders, documents, and data accessible to all case workers at any time. There is no standard notation for the case file, although file items whose lifecycle events trigger plan item entry and exit conditions are depicted graphically in the case plan.

- *Case roles* are used to define authorized performers of case tasks and to control permissions for certain other actions. Case role definitions are not visualized in the diagram.

When we speak of the *CMMN diagram*, we mean specifically the *case plan model*. The details of the case file and case roles are exposed to stakeholders who are not case authors only through the *case documentation* generated by the tool.

Communicating Case Logic

CMMN logic is more difficult to communicate visually than is BPMN logic. There are two reasons for this. The first reason is its lack of familiarity. When BPMN was first created, its designers intentionally copied the basic elements of swimlane flowcharts, the diagrams most often used by businesspeople to describe their processes. Thus, BPMN diagrams were familiar-looking to business from the start. CMMN, in contrast, intentionally made its notation *different*, not just different from BPMN but different from anything businesspeople have ever seen.

The second reason is inherent in the declarative paradigm. Most people find procedural description of process logic – the BPMN way – far easier to follow than declarative. What happens first? In BPMN that's the *start event*. What determines when this section of processing is complete? That's an *end event*, and in Method and Style the end event label names the *end state*. What happens in what order? In BPMN, that's what *sequence flow*, the solid arrow, is for.

CMMN, in contrast, has no start events, no end events, no sequence flow, and no defined end states. Part of the reason is there is often no single defined start action or completing action. It could be that a section of the case – a *stage* – is complete only when a case worker decides to call it complete. So increased flexibility in what can happen in what order makes visual communication of the logic inherently more difficult.

Aside from purely human decisions, what drives the case logic forward are *events* based on *lifecycle state transitions* of *case plan items* – tasks, stages, and milestones – and of *case file items* – data and documents. In order to understand CMMN, it is necessary to understand the *lifecycle states* of plan items and file items and the *standard events* that transition from one state to the next. Both are standardized in the CMMN spec. State diagrams are admittedly harder for businesspeople to understand, but to comprehend CMMN there is no way around it.

Another reason, of course, is the lack of attention in the spec to ensuring that elements important to understanding the case logic are clearly revealed in the diagrams. Like the BPMN 2.0 spec, the CMMN spec is so focused on operational semantics – ensuring executability on an automation engine – that it neglects what is more important to most modelers, ensuring that the logic is expressed clearly and completely from the printed diagrams alone. That's where Method and Style comes in. Method and Style is a system of conventions called *style rules*, layered on top of the rules of the spec, intended to make the meaning of the logic evident from the printed diagram.

While a case automation engine can access detailed properties of model elements defined in the tool, most stakeholders cannot see those. They see only what is printed in the diagram. Any properties important for understanding the behavior must be captured somehow in the diagram, through labels, symbols, and when necessary, text annotations. While the CMMN spec defines many of those things, like BPMN 2.0 it does not insist that modelers use them. Method and Style says you *must* use them, and defines validation rules based on those requirements.

Because CMMN logic is inherently difficult to communicate visually, standard conventions like Method and Style are needed to give case management stakeholders a fighting chance of understanding what is going on.

The Method and Style conventions are my own, not part of the standard. They began with BPMN and have been carried over to DMN and now CMMN. In Trisotech's CMMN tool, models can be checked automatically for conformance to the style rules. The style rules for CMMN are discussed in Chapter 7.

CHAPTER 2

Case Plan Elements

The case plan model is a set of diagrams and associated dialogs that define which actions may be performed in the case at any time. The case plan model as a whole is depicted as a tabbed folder (Figure 2). The label in the tab is the name of the case model (NOT the case instance, e.g. client name). This shape is also implicitly the top-level stage in the case.

All plan items for the case are contained in the case plan model. Figure 2 illustrates many of them.

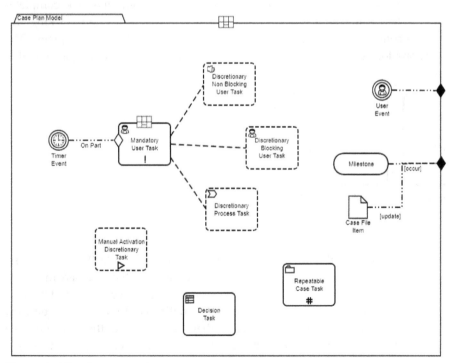

Figure 2. Plan item notation

Like BPMN models, CMMN case plan models are implicitly *hierarchical*. Similar to subprocesses in BPMN, CMMN *stages* are containers of other plan items, and may be rendered either collapsed or expanded. In the tool, a diagram containing a *collapsed* stage is hyperlinked to a child-level diagram displaying the *expanded* view of the stage and its contained plan items. This allows complex case plan models to be organized as a hierarchy of diagrams, allowing both high-level and detailed views of case behavior within the context of a single case plan definition.

Tasks

Tasks are actions performed in the case. They are represented in the diagram as rounded rectangles. The *task label* identifies the action, best specified as Verb-object. The icon in the upper left corner indicates the type of task.

User Task

The head-and-shoulders icon identifies a *blocking user task*. *Blocking* means that once the task starts, the stage containing the task may not complete until the task completes or terminates (and no other contained plan items are active). *User task* means the task is performed by a person, the case worker.

The hand icon identifies a *non-blocking user task*. *Non-blocking* means the task completes immediately upon activation, even if the action it initiates takes longer. A non-blocking task does not require its containing stage to wait for the non-blocking action to complete. The principal use for non-blocking user tasks is documentation, indicating something is done that is not captured by a system.

Figure 3. Blocking and Non-blocking User task

Case Task

The white folder icon identifies a *blocking case task*. A case task initiates ("calls") a CMMN case. Although the called case is nominally independent of the calling case, the case task may pass as much or as little of the parent case file to the called case, allowing it to be referenced by logic in the called case, or "subcase". The called case returns via its defined outputs the data returned to the calling case. The advantage of using a case task rather than a stage for this purpose is the called case may run either standalone or as a subcase, while a stage can only be part of a larger case.

Method and Style indicates *non-blocking case tasks* with a black folder icon. Here the calling case does not wait for the called case to complete. A case communicates with an already running instance of another case not by using a case task but via *file items* shared by the two cases.

Figure 4. Blocking and Non-blocking Case task

Process Task

The white chevron icon identifies a *blocking process task*. The task initiates a BPMN process modeled externally to the case. In tools like Trisotech and Flowable, the process task hyperlinks to the invoked process model. Again, blocking means the stage containing the task may not complete until the called process is complete.

The spec says *non-blocking process tasks* are those without defined *outputs*, one of those detailed properties that are not shown in the diagram. For that reason, Method and Style indicates non-blocking process tasks with a black chevron. Non-blocking means the stage containing the task may complete before the called process is complete. Like a case task, a process task may pass as much or as little of its case file information to the called process as it chooses, and receives back any process outputs.

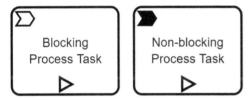

Figure 5. Blocking and Non-blocking Process task

Decision Task

The spreadsheet icon identifies a *decision task*, which calls a DMN decision service. In Trisotech and Flowable the called DMN model is hyperlinked to the calling task. Since decision services are short-running, a decision task is always blocking.

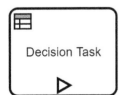

Figure 6. Decision task

Generic Task

A task with no task type icon is a *generic task*. Its specific type and whether blocking or non-blocking are undefined. It has pedagogical purpose in illustrating behavior common to all task types, but in real CMMN models it is not normally used.

Figure 7. Generic task

Task Roles

A task may be assigned to one or more *case roles*, meaning only case workers in that role may perform the task or declare it complete. The assigned role is not visualized in the diagram, although a tool could provide it, for example, as an overlay.

Discretionary Tasks

A task with a dashed border signifies a *discretionary task*. The name threw me off for quite a while. It should be called a *conditional task*, because it means that the task may be instantiated only in certain case instances, as determined by rules defined at design time. These so-called *applicability rules* are Boolean expressions of case data (file items). In addition, discretionary items specify *authorization rules* that determine which case roles may instantiate the item.

Figure 8. Discretionary task

Since the applicability rules are Boolean expressions of case file items, their value changes as the case progresses. If all applicability rules for a discretionary task are true, then an authorized case worker may at runtime instantiate the discretionary task in the case instance. In the spec this is called *planning*, even though it occurs dynamically at runtime.

A discretionary item's *context* is either its containing stage or a human task with a dashed connector link to it. We say the item is "discretionary to the context." For example, in Figure 9, the context for discretionary task *Y* is task *X*, and the context for discretionary task *Z* is stage *S*. (A discretionary task with no dashed links to another task is discretionary to its containing stage.) The context must be active in order for a discretionary item to be available.

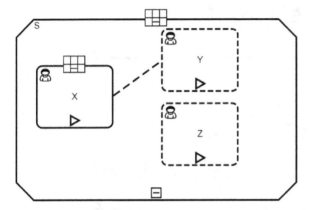

Figure 9. Context for discretionary items

A task or stage that is the context for a discretionary item contains a *planning table,* a small grid icon on the top boundary. If the bottom center cell in the grid has a minus (-), the discretionary items are displayed in the diagram. If that cell has a plus (+), the discretionary items are hidden. Opening the planning table lists the applicability and authorization rules for each discretionary item.

Stages

A *stage* (rectangle with beveled corners) represents a phase or state of a case. It serves as a *container* of plan items (tasks, nested stages, milestones, and event listeners). As mentioned previously, the case plan model (folder shape) is the top-level stage of the case. All other stages are represented graphically as a rectangle with clipped corners.

Like a subprocess in BPMN, a stage may be represented in two ways (Figure 10):

- *Expanded,* a resizable shape enclosing its contained plan items, with a [-] marker bottom center, or

- *Collapsed,* an opaque shape, with a [+] marker bottom center. Typically, in a CMMN tool a collapsed stage is hyperlinked to its expanded representation on a child-level page, similar to subprocesses in BPMN.

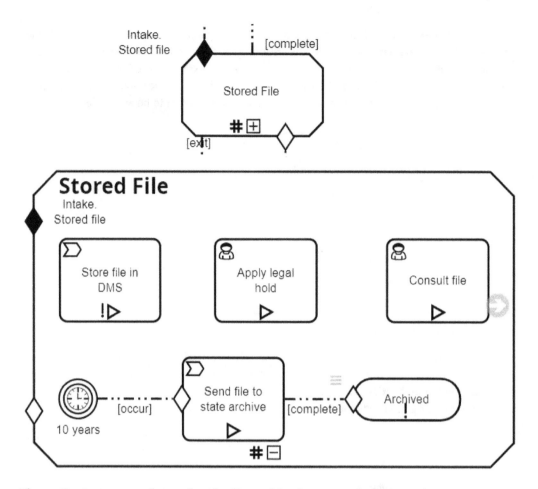

Figure 10. A stage may be rendered collapsed (top) or expanded (bottom)

Stages are important elements determining which tasks are *Available* to start at what phase of the case. For example, a task does not become *Available* until its containing stage becomes *Active* and becomes *Terminated* automatically if its containing stage terminates. *Available, Active, Completed,* and *Terminated* are defined *lifecycle states* of all tasks and stages. More than one stage may be *Active* at the same time, although it is possible to design case plans in which only one stage (besides the case plan model as a whole) is *Active* at any time. We'll explain case behavior in detail later in this chapter.

Collapsed stage representations are useful in modeling complex cases as a hierarchy of diagrams. Each collapsed stage in the top-level diagram is hyperlinked to a child-level diagram containing the expanded stage representation, and if that child diagram contains other collapsed stages, there are additional child diagrams.

In simple case plan models, it is common to see only expanded stages, with the entire case plan model captured in a single diagram. In those models it is also common to see *links* – connectors representing event-triggered behavior – that cross the boundary of an expanded stage.

However, such links cannot be represented in hierarchical case models, since there is no valid way to represent the link to or from an item contained in the collapsed stage.[4] *For that reason, Method and Style deprecates use of event links that cross a stage boundary,* even though these are often seen in CMMN diagrams.

Discretionary Stages

Like tasks, stages may be *discretionary*, indicated by a dashed boundary. The context for a discretionary stage is its containing stage, which controls instantiation via its planning table. The same mechanism of applicability rules and authorization rules applies for both discretionary stages and discretionary tasks.

Case Behavior Overview

Unlike BPMN, in which progress is described procedurally as a chain of sequence flows, CMMN logic is *declarative*. That means that each plan item independently defines its own requirements for when it starts or is enabled to start, when it is able to complete, and when it is forced to terminate. In addition to *automated* behavior based on events and data conditions, plan items often may be started, completed, or terminated *manually* by case workers. While this combination gives great flexibility to the possible order of case actions, it makes the possibilities considerably more challenging to communicate visually through a diagram.

Case behavior as defined in the CMMN spec is based on a *lifecycle state model* of tasks and stages, in which *state transitions* generate *events* that trigger actions and other state transitions. We'll go through that in detail later, but because it is an unfamiliar and possibly daunting way to understand process behavior, the following overview should help you with the big picture.

To understand a CMMN diagram, the key questions for any task or stage in the diagram are when does it start, when can it complete, and when is forced to terminate. Here is how to think about that.

Starting

A *stage* is a container for *tasks* and other stages. The general rule is that a task or stage is *Available* when its containing stage is in the *Active* state, meaning the containing stage is started and not yet completed or terminated. If the task or stage is marked *Manually Activated*, once *Available* it waits in the *Enabled* state until manually started by a case worker. Without that marker, start is automatic, meaning it becomes *Active* immediately when its containing stage becomes *Active*.

---

[4] This differs from BPMN, in which a message flow drawn to or from a collapsed subprocess in a parent diagram must be replicated as a message flow drawn directly to or from a contained item in the expanded child diagram. Such semantics for event links are not defined in the CMMN spec.

The above is true unless the *Available* task or stage has one or more *entry conditions*, denoted by a white diamond-shaped *sentry* on its border. In that case, in addition to the containing stage being *Active*, the entry condition – based on a triggering *event* and possibly a *data condition* – must be satisfied.

The triggering event is a *lifecycle state transition* of some other plan item or file item. Occurrence of the event dictates *when* the data condition is tested. The condition, a Boolean expression of case file item values at the time of the triggering event, dictates *whether* the task or stage is enabled. If no triggering event, called the sentry's *ON-part*, is specified, the condition is tested when the containing stage becomes *Active*. If no data condition, called the sentry's *IF-part*, is specified, the condition is considered satisfied by default, and the task or stage is enabled whenever the triggering event occurs. When its entry condition is satisfied, a task or stage marked *Manually Activated* waits in the *Enabled* state for manual start by a case worker.

It's easy to get lost in the details, but the key thing to remember is that most tasks – and many stages, as well – are *Manually Activated* and, once enabled, must be started manually by a case worker. In case management software based on executable CMMN, depending on the currently *Active* stage or stages, **the list of tasks and stages awaiting manual start defines a menu of available actions at runtime.** In fact, such a menu is typically part of the runtime user interface in CMMN applications.

Completing

After performing its actions, a task or stage moves from the *Active* state to either *Completed* or *Terminated*. *Completed* generally implies success and *Terminated* implies failure, but this is not necessarily true.

A user task determines for itself when it is *Completed*, but that is not true for a stage. With minor exceptions, a stage may be *Completed* – either automatically or manually by a case worker – only when none of its contained tasks and stages are *Active*, and any contained plan items marked *Required* are either *Completed* or *Terminated*. Contained non-*Required* tasks awaiting manual start do not inhibit marking the stage *Completed*.

The *complete* event of a task or stage, signifying it has reached the *Completed* state, is frequently used to trigger entry conditions of other plan items. The case logic, however, may require more detail, such as *how* did the task or stage complete, in what *end state*? Method and Style uses *milestones* to indicate the end state of a stage. Technically a milestone is a type of *event*, used in the ON-part of an entry or exit condition. However, Method and Style assumes each occurring milestone is captured in an *implicit file item* for use in sentry IF-part conditions. The *complete* event of a task or stage in combination with its end state as revealed by this file item is a common logic pattern in CMMN Method and Style.

Terminating

CMMN places restrictions on when a task or stage may be *Completed*, but it also allows an *Active* task or stage to be *Terminated* manually at any time by a case worker. More often, however, an *exit condition* of the task or stage, denoted by a *black sentry* on its boundary, models *automatic* termination of the task or stage based on events and data conditions. While both manual and automated termination take the task or stage to the *Terminated* state, they generate different events. Manual termination generates the *terminate* event, while automated termination generates the *exit* event.

Case Behavior and the Task/Stage Lifecycle

As mentioned in the previous discussion, every plan item follows a standard *lifecycle*, defined in the spec as a *state diagram*, progressing from one lifecycle state to another by a combination of case worker actions and events. That means, for example, an *Available* task or stage *starts* (moves to the *Active* state) when its preconditions *allow* it to start and, if marked *Manually Activated*, it is manually started by a case worker. Similar logic determines when a task or stage *completes* (moves to the *Completed* state) or *exits* (moves to the *Terminated* state).

Moreover, every lifecycle state transition generates a *standard event* that may be used to trigger transitions of other plan items. Basing the start or completion of plan items on a combination of ad-hoc user action and events allows tremendous flexibility in what can happen when – much more than BPMN allows – but, not surprisingly, it makes clear visual communication of case logic more challenging.

Lifecycle State Model

The lifecycle states of a task or stage are shown in Figure 11.

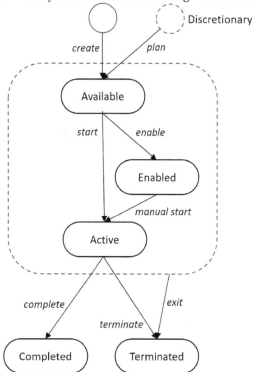

Figure 11. Lifecycle states of a task or stage

In this diagram, the lifecycle *states* are the ovals, their names capitalized, and the *transitions* between then are the arrows, their names not capitalized. Each transition represents a *standard event* that can be used to trigger other case behavior.

The top circle labeled *Discretionary* and associated transition labeled *plan* are not named as such in the spec. I added them to the diagram to illustrate how discretionary tasks and stages fit into the lifecycle state model. Normal (non-discretionary) tasks and stages begin at the unlabeled circle, meaning not yet *Available*. As a case progresses, plan items evolve from this state to *Available*, *Enabled*, *Active*, and ultimately to either *Completed* or *Terminated*.

In the spec, this diagram includes also the states *Disabled*, *Failed*, and *Suspended*, which represent temporary runtime exceptions, but in this book, we focus on the design-time states: *Available*, *Enabled*, *Active*, *Completed*, and *Terminated*.

Available

A non-discretionary task or stage transitions from the unlabeled state to *Available* (signaled as a *create* event)…

- … when its containing stage becomes *Active*. The containing stage for a plan item not enclosed by any stage shape is the case as a whole, which is always manually activated.

A discretionary task or stage becomes *Available* …

- … upon manual user action, if its containing stage is *Active* and such action is allowed by the planning table.

Enabled

A *Manually Activated* task or stage transitions from *Available* to *Enabled* (*enable* event)…

- … upon satisfaction of an entry condition, OR
- … immediately, if it has no entry conditions.

Active

A *Manually Activated* task or stage transitions from *Enabled* to *Active* (*manual start* event)…

- … when started manually by a case worker.

A task or stage that is NOT *Manually Activated* transitions from *Available* to *Active* (*start* event)…

- … upon satisfaction of an entry condition, OR
- … immediately, if it has no entry conditions.

Completed

A *blocking user task* transitions from *Active* to *Completed* (*complete* event)…

- … *manually* when declared complete by a case worker.

A *decision task* or *blocking case or process task* transitions from *Active* to *Completed*…

- … *automatically* when the decision, case, or process completes.

A *non-blocking user, case, or process task* transitions from *Active* to *Completed*…

- … immediately.

A *stage* transitions from *Active* to *Completed*…

- … *automatically* when marked *Autocomplete* AND no contained plan items are *Active* AND all contained plan items marked *Required* are *Completed* or *Terminated*.

- … *manually* by case worker action when no contained plan items are *Active* AND all contained plan items marked *Required* are either *Completed* or *Terminated*.

Terminated

A task or stage transitions from *Available, Enabled,* or *Active* to *Terminated* (*exit* event)…

- … *automatically* when an exit condition of the task or stage becomes true.

- … *automatically* when its containing stage transitions to *Terminated*.

A task or stage transitions from *Active* to *Terminated* (*terminate* event)…

- … *manually* by case worker action.

Entry and Exit Conditions

In many cases, transitions to the *Active* and *Terminated* states are controlled by entry and exit conditions of the plan item. In the model these are represented by diamond-shapes called *sentries*, placed on the plan item boundary. A white sentry indicates an entry condition; a black sentry indicates an exit condition.

Event-Condition-Action

Sentries are CMMN's representation of the *event-condition-action* pattern. An *event* is a change of lifecycle state of a plan item or file item. Sentries listen for specific events, as specified by their *ON-parts*. The CMMN spec enumerates a number of *standard events* for each type of plan item and for file items. The standard events of a plan item are the lifecycle state transitions shown in Figure 11 and discussed in the previous section. The standard events of a file item will be discussed in the next chapter.

A sentry may have zero or more ON-parts. In the diagram, each ON-part is visualized as a *link* – a dash-dot connector – from the triggering item boundary to the sentry, labeled with the triggering event. A sentry with multiple ON-parts means *all* of the triggers must occur before evaluating the IF-part. If no ON-part link is displayed, the triggering event is activation of the containing stage. [Note: One end of the link MUST connect to a plan item or file item boundary and the other MUST connect to a sentry. **Links from one sentry to another, which you sometimes see, are invalid!**]

Regardless of the number of ON-part links, each sentry has exactly one *IF-part*, indicating *whether* entry or exit occurs. The IF-part is a *condition*, a Boolean expression of file item values, evaluated when triggered by the ON-part. In Method and Style, the sentry's IF-part is visualized as the *sentry label*. If the sentry has no label, the IF-part condition is *true* by default.

Since Method and Style prohibits ON-part links from outside the containing stage, the containing stage must be *Active* – and thus the plan item with the sentry must be *Available* – in order for the ON-part link to have effect. A sentry's ON-part determines *when* to evaluate the IF-part. Upon evaluation, the IF-part determines *whether* to perform the action.

For a white sentry, that action transitions the plan item either to *Enabled or Active,* depending on whether or not the item is *Manually Activated.* For a black sentry, the action transitions the plan item to *Terminated.*

ANDed vs ORed Conditions

A single sentry with multiple ON-parts ANDs those events, meaning it waits for all of them to occur and evaluates its IF-part when the last event occurs. For example, in Figure 12, task *d* becomes *Enabled* when task *b* is *complete* AND task *c* is *complete*. Here no label on the sentry means the IF-part is true by default.

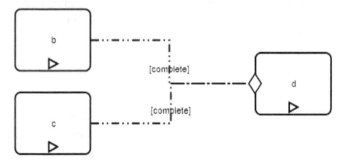

Figure 12. ANDed entry criteria

When a plan item has multiple entry conditions (white sentries), any one of them may trigger the *Available* state. In other words, the entry conditions are ORed. Similarly, when a plan item has multiple exit conditions (black sentries), any one of them may trigger the *Terminated* state. For example, in Figure 13, task *d* becomes *Enabled* either when task *b* completes OR task *c* completes, whichever comes first.

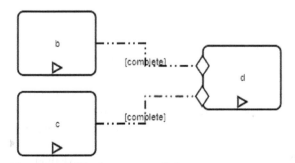

Figure 13. ORed entry conditions

Links May Not Cross Stage Boundary

In Method and Style, sentry ON-part links may not cross a stage boundary. The CMMN spec makes contradictory statements about entry criteria crossing a stage boundary. In one place it forbids such links; in another it says such a link "wakes up" the containing stage, making it *Available* along with its containing stage, if any, and implicitly its contained plan items as well.

It is a bug in the spec, as both statements cannot be true simultaneously.[5] In this book we follow the first one: ***Sentry ON-part links MAY NOT cross a stage boundary.*** In Method and Style, at least, such a link is an error.

Hierarchical models further justify the rule that ON-part links may not cross a stage boundary, as there is no way to indicate connection across the stage boundary when the stage is collapsed.

Violations of this rule are quite common, including diagrams in the CMMN spec itself. We will see how to correct this and other style errors in Chapter 7.

Stage Representation in Hierarchical Models

When a collapsed stage has entry and/or exit sentries, the expanded stage representation on a child page of the model must replicate the sentry shape and its label. In the parent diagram containing the collapsed stage, only links from outside the stage are depicted. In the child diagram containing the expanded stage, only links from inside the stage are depicted.

Control Symbols

As suggested in the previous discussion, some plan item behavior is controlled by plan item attributes depicted as symbols at the bottom center of the shape. (In the spec these are called "decorators".)

Manual Activation

The *Manual Activation* symbol ▷ means the plan item transitions automatically from *Available* to *Enabled*, where it awaits *manual start* by a case worker. Only then does it become *Active*. Without the symbol, the plan item becomes *Active* (*start* event) automatically as soon as it becomes *Available*.

---

[5] One was a rule of CMMN 1.0. The other was added in CMMN 1.1, but the old rule was not deleted from the spec. Regardless, the semantics of an event outside the containing stage enabling a not-yet-*Available* plan item, making it and its containing stage *Available* and all sibling plan items likewise *Available*, is inconsistent with CMMN semantics generally. For this reason, in Method and Style a link originating outside the containing stage is explicitly not allowed.

Required

The *Required* symbol ! means the plan item must be *Completed* (or *Terminated*) before its containing stage may be *Completed*. Without the symbol, completion of the plan item is *optional*, meaning its containing stage may be declared *Completed* as long as the plan item is not *Active* and all other completion conditions of the stage are met. A typical use of *Required* is to ensure that the containing stage cannot become *Completed* until the item is either *Completed* or *Terminated*.

Autocomplete

The *Autocomplete* symbol ■ on a stage means the stage becomes *Completed* automatically when all of its *Required* plan items are *Completed* or *Terminated* and no contained plan items are *Active*. In Figure 14, stage *S* autocompletes when *Required* task *A* is *Completed* or *Terminated*, unless task *B* is *Active*. Without *Autocomplete*, the stage must be completed manually.

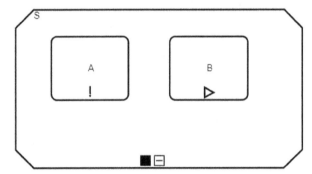

Figure 14. Autocomplete marker

Modelers should use *Autocomplete* with care. A stage marked *Autocomplete* with all tasks *Manually Activated* should have at least one plan item marked *Required* or the stage could complete unexpectedly. For example, in Figure 15, stage *S* autocompletes as soon as it is started, since it has no *Required* or *Active* plan items.

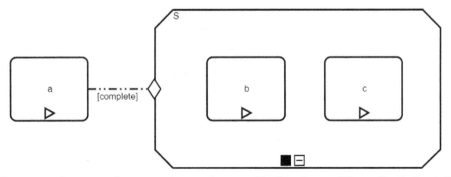

Figure 15. *Autocomplete* stage is a style error if all tasks are *Manually Activated* and there are no *Required* plan items in the stage

Repeatable

The *Repeatable* symbol **#** means multiple instances of the plan item may be created, subject to a *Repetition Rule*, a Boolean expression of file item values. The Repetition Rule is evaluated when the plan item completes or terminates, and if the rule evaluates to true a new instance of the plan item becomes *Available*. In Method and Style, a Repetition Rule, if it exists, is visualized as a text annotation. In a *Repeatable* plan item with no such text annotation, the Repetition Rule is always true by default.

If a *Repeatable* plan item with no entry condition is *Manually Activated*, the new instance automatically becomes *Enabled* upon *complete* or *exit*. If it is NOT *Manually Activated*, it automatically becomes *Active* upon *complete* or *exit*.

If a *Repeatable* plan item has an entry condition, every occurrence of its ON-part event creates a new instance of the plan item, even if the previous instance is still *Active*. Normally such an entry condition is triggered from another *Repeatable* plan item. The spec says an entry condition in a *Repeatable* plan item must contain an ON-part. That implies that to specify looping or multi-instance behavior of the plan item, you should use a Repetition Rule. This is illustrated with examples in Chapter 8.

Behavior Property Rules

Technically, the behaviors implied by the *Repeatable, Required,* and *Autocomplete* symbols only apply if their associated *behavior property rule* is true. This rule is an optional Boolean expression of file item values. Quite often there is no associated behavior property rule and the implied behavior applies by default. If a behavior property rule exists, Method and Style requires it to be visualized in a text annotation linked to the plan item.

Milestones

A *milestone* is a plan item denoting achievement of a named state of the stage or case. It is depicted as an oval shape and is best labeled Adjective or Noun-Adjective to indicate the state. The lifecycle state diagram for a milestone is shown in Figure 16.

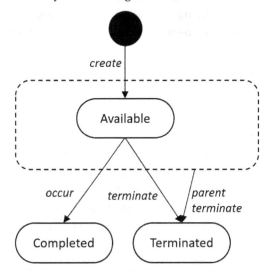

Figure 16. Lifecycle states of a milestone or event listener

A milestone becomes *Available* when its containing stage is *Active*. In the *Available* state, a milestone awaits triggering by its entry criteria (*occur* event), at which point it becomes *Completed*. An *Available* milestone with no entry criteria may be *Completed* by manual case worker action. It becomes *Terminated* either when its containing stage becomes *Terminated* or upon manual case worker action. A milestone also may be marked *Required* and/or *Repeatable*.

A milestone affects case behavior in two ways:

- Its *occur* event may be linked to entry or exit criteria of other plan items. In Method and Style, those links may not cross a stage boundary. For example, in Figure 17, the milestone *X Started* is triggered when task *X* becomes *Active*. This in turn triggers task *Y* to start.

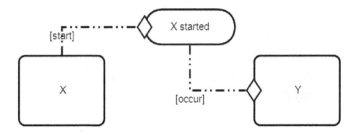

Figure 17. Milestones are triggered by events and can trigger other plan items

- Method and Style further assumes that the current *state* of each milestone (i.e., *Completed* or not) is captured in an implicit file item *Milestones*, referenceable by conditional logic in the case plan, such as the IF-part of an entry or exit condition of other plan items. Since file items are global, these plan items are not required to be in the same stage as the milestone. The *Milestones* file item is a list of the names of all milestones currently in the *Completed* state, with the format [*stage name*].[*milestone name*]. This means the names of milestones must be unique within a stage but not unique across the entire case.

Marking a milestone as *Required* is a way to ensure that a stage cannot complete until the milestone's entry condition is satisfied.

Milestone as Stage Variable

Persisting the current state of all case milestones in a file item, as described above, allows them to play a part in CMMN Method and Style similar to *end events* in BPMN Method and Style,[6] where they indicate distinct *end states* of a process or subprocess. In BPMN Method and Style, a subprocess's end state value is the end event name and is normally tested by a gateway in the flow branching logic, each gate labeled with a different end state. This makes the process logic clear from the printed diagrams without requiring explicit definition of process variables.

CMMN Method and Style borrows this idea. In CMMN, milestones similarly represent *states achieved by the containing stage*, although – as in Figure 17 – they do not necessarily signify the *final* state of the stage, merely a state achieved during the stage. Also, unlike end states in BPMN Method and Style, milestones are not necessarily *distinct* states. In fact, it is common for a stage to have more than one milestone in the *Completed* state.

Persisting the list of *Completed* milestones in the implicit file item *Milestones* allows the state of a particular milestone to be tested by a sentry IF-part even if that sentry is outside the containing stage of the milestone. In Method and Style, this is the basic mechanism for controlling which plan items are triggered following completion of a stage based on its end state. Many examples of this are illustrated in Chapter 8.

Event Listeners

In addition to standard transitions of tasks, stages, and file items, plan item entry and exit criteria may be triggered by an *event listener*. Event listeners are depicted in the case plan model as double rings, like BPMN intermediate events.

The lifecycle states of an event listener are shown in Figure 16. Event listeners have no entry or exit criteria, but their *occur* events (*Completed* state) may trigger entry or exit of other plan items. Like milestones, an *Available* (not yet *Completed*) event listener may transition to the *Terminated*

---

[6] Bruce Silver, BPMN Method and Style 2nd edition, https://www.amazon.com/dp/0982368119

state either by manual case worker action (*terminate* event) or automatically when its parent stage terminates (*parent terminate* event).

Timer Event Listener

A *timer event listener*, with a clock icon inside, models a time delay or deadline. Its properties include the *start trigger*, a standard event of a specified plan item or file item; and a *timer expression*, either a duration, a specified date/time, or a repeating interval.[7] The spec provides no visual indication of the start trigger, so Method and Style provides one in the form of an annotation. In Method and Style, the start trigger is indicated by a *directional association* (dotted line connector with arrow) from the triggering item to the event listener, labeled with the standard event. If no start trigger is specified – in Method and Style, signified by the absence of this directional association – the start trigger is activation of the containing stage. The timer expression is indicated in the diagram by the event listener label. For example (Figure 18), task X is enabled 1 day after stage S becomes *Active*, and task Y is enabled 1 hour after task X becomes *Completed*.

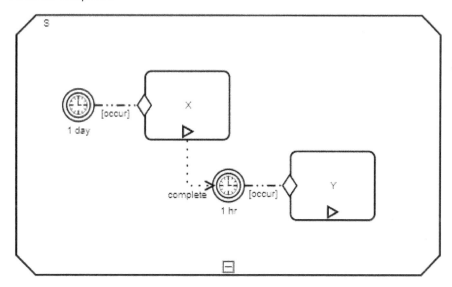

Figure 18. Timer event listeners

User Event Listener

A *user event listener*, with a head-and-shoulders icon inside, represents manual triggering by a case worker. It is typically used to enable manual triggering of plan items containing other event-based entry or exit criteria. The CMMN spec provides no defined meaning for the label

---

[7] Although the spec does not define event listeners as *Repeatable*, a repeating interval timer expression implies repeatability. In Method and Style, event listeners are implicitly *Repeatable*.

of a user event listener. In Method and Style, the event listener label typically identifies the source of a human-mediated event, such as "Further investigation required".[8]

For example (Figure 19), task Y is enabled either 1 hour after completion of task X or manually upon the action of a case worker, whichever comes first, meaning *no later than* 1 hour after completion of task X.

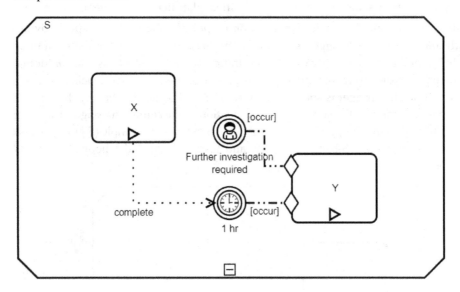

Figure 19. User event listener

---

[8] As stated previously, in Method and Style, event listeners are implicitly *Repeatable*, so a user event listener may *occur* more than once.

File Item Triggers

Although they are not plan items, *file items* whose lifecycle events trigger plan item behavior are represented in the case plan model by a document icon linked to the sentry of the triggered plan item. As with plan item events, the link is labeled with the name of the file item standard event, enclosed in brackets. The file item lifecycle and standard events are discussed in Chapter 3.

When a plan item acts upon a file item, Method and Style visualizes this in the diagram with a directional association from the plan item to the file item, labeled with the name of the action. For example (Figure 20), task X creates the file item *contract*, as indicated by the directional association. This file item standard event (*create*) triggers enablement of task Y, indicated by the ON-part link.

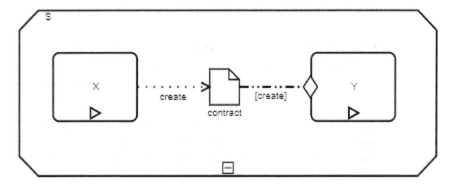

Figure 20. File item creation (non-normative) and file item trigger

File items are global – not local to a stage – so ON-part links from a file item event are exempt from the rule about crossing stage boundaries. However, the triggered plan item must be *Available* to be enabled by the link.

Diagram Annotations

In addition to plan items and file item transitions, the CMMN diagram may also contain annotations that help explain the logic but have no direct execution semantics. In the spec these are called *artifacts*. They include *text annotations* and *associations*.

Text Annotation

A *text annotation* is modeler-entered text enclosed in a square left bracket linked to a plan item by a dotted line connector called an *association* (Figure 21). This is the same text annotation shape used in BPMN and DMN. Method and Style may require a text annotation to suggest model behavior not otherwise reflected in the diagram. Examples include:

- Presence of a behavior property rule
- Looping or multi-instance behavior

- Clarification of an entry or exit condition

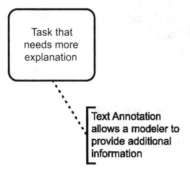

Figure 21. Text annotation adds explanatory information to the diagram

Association

An *association* is a dotted line connector used as a diagram annotation. The shape is distinguished from an ON-part link (dash-dot) and a discretionary task link (dashed) connector. An association may optionally include a V-shaped arrowhead at one end, called a *directional association*.

In Method and Style, creation, update, or deletion of a file item by a task may be depicted in the diagram as a directional association from the task to a file item icon, as we saw in Figure 20. Also, a directional association is used to indicate the start trigger of a timer event listener, as shown in Figure 18.

Labels

In executable models, certain details determining case behavior are specified by modelers in dialog boxes in the tool, but a key assumption of Method and Style is that other stakeholders do not have access to those dialog boxes. The only information available to them is what is displayed in the diagrams. In that context, *labels* assume great importance.

For certain labels CMMN defines the meaning. For example, the label of a task or stage is its *name*. An ON-part link label, enclosed in square brackets, specifies a *standard event* of the plan item or file item at the tail end of the link. In many other cases, however, the spec does not specify a particular meaning to a label. Such labels have no direct execution semantics but may be used to *suggest* execution semantics defined in dialog boxes.

Method and Style *requires* such labels in certain situations. For example:

- The label of a sentry suggests the IF-part condition. No label means no IF-part condition exists.

- Similarly, the label of an association from a task to a file item indicates the operation of the plan item on the file item: create, update, delete, etc.

- The label of a timer event listener suggests its timer expression.

CHAPTER 3

Case File Model

The *case file model* defines the *file items* – data and documents – collected and used in the case. File item content and metadata inform case workers as they perform tasks. Like plan items, file items have defined *lifecycle states*. *Standard events*, representing lifecycle state transitions, are used in the case plan in the same way plan item events are, as ON-part triggers of plan item entry and exit conditions.

Unless restricted by access control in the case file repository, all case file items are assumed to be available to any case worker at any time. Case file items include both content and data, although in the spec the emphasis is on content. *Content items* – documents and folders – include *metadata* (name, document type, last modified date, etc.) in addition to the actual content, which is often an "unstructured" document, meaning human-readable but not necessarily processable by case logic. CMMN's emphasis on associating case file items with content rather than data is largely historical – as mentioned earlier, the reaction of document workflow vendors against the SOA orientation of BPMN 2.0 – but it is not actually fundamental. In this book, we use case file items to represent both data and content.

Case Variables as File Items

Executable modeling depends on *variables* defined in the tool, typically by programmers, and often not visualized in the diagrams. Method and Style tries to make the case logic visible in the diagrams, and for that reason assumes that case variables – at least those related to progression of the case plan – are represented by *file items,* since file item events used in the case plan model are captured visually in the diagrams.

This means that in Method and Style, any file item may serve as a *case variable* used in the case plan model and, conversely, any case variable is a file item. For example, expressions of file item data and metadata are used in IF-part of entry and exit conditions. In some CMMN tools, case variables are distinct from file items, but defining all variables as file items allows them to be visually represented in the diagrams.

Case File Item Definition Type

Although the CMMN spec defines standard attributes for case file items, the way they are specified and implemented is different in each CMMN product. In this book we follow the approach taken by Trisotech, which uses FEEL as a common expression language across BPMN, DMN, and CMMN. [9] Each case file item has a *name*, a *file item definition type*, and a *structureRef*, a pointer to the data definition. In Trisotech Case Modeler, the case file item definition types include *data, document,* and *folder,* and the *structureRef* names a FEEL datatype.

For data, FEEL base types are Text, Number, Boolean, Date, Time, DateTime, DayTimeDuration, and YearMonthDuration. If a case file item is one of these types without constraints, the structureRef names the base type. For structured data, collections, and base types with constraints, a custom user-defined type called an *item definition* must be specified[10]. Structured data, like a database record, consists of *components,* each with a defined type. For numbers and calendar types, constraints typically are minimum and maximum values. For text types, constraints are typically enumerated values. In addition, an item definition may be specified as a *collection* of another type, either a base type or another item definition. For example, a table is a collection of the item definition for the row type, a structure with a component for each table column.

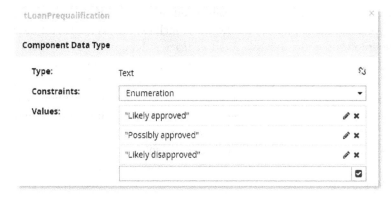

Figure 22. File item datatype with enumerated values

For example (Figure 22), the item definition tLoanPrequalification is the FEEL base type Text with enumerated values "Likely approved", "Possibly approved", and "Likely disapproved".

---

[9] FEEL is a business-friendly data type and expression language defined in the DMN spec but used by Trisotech across all three business automation languages. Other tools, like Flowable, use Java's Expression Language across those three languages, but as Method and Style focuses on the needs of business users rather than programmers, this book assumes FEEL.

[10] The nomenclature is confusing: *Case file item definition* comes from the CMMN spec. The *item definition* pointed to by *structureRef* is from the FEEL spec and not the same thing. It is effectively an attribute of the case file item definition.

In Figure 23, the item definition tCreditScore is FEEL base type Number constrained to the range 300 to 850 inclusive. The item definition editor defines the types with those constraints.

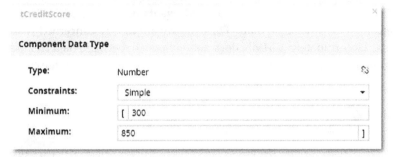

Figure 23. File item datatype with allowed values in numeric range

For documents and folders, Trisotech offers a datatype *Document*, a structure with the following components:[11]

- *Name* (text): Document Name (filename)
- *Created* (date and time): Document creation date
- *Last Modified* (date and Time: Document last modification date
- *Size* (number): size of the document
- *Type* (text): mime-type or equivalent
- *URL* (text): URL to retrieve the document

---

[11] Details are subject to change.

File Item Lifecycle

Like plan items, file items have a standard lifecycle (Figure 24). All standard events except *delete* leave the file item in the *Available* state. The standard events defined in the spec are oriented to documents and folders rather than data. For data, we are mostly concerned with the *create* and *update* events. Unfortunately, CMMN does not distinguish between data created in the case and received from outside, like a BPMN message. Both are represented by the *create* event.

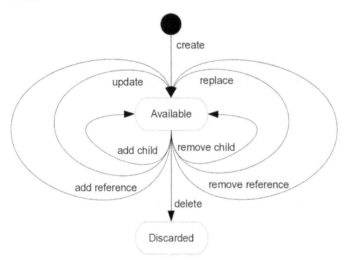

Figure 24. Lifecycle states of a file item

Method and Style: Implicit File Items and Related Case Logic

Like BPMN models, CMMN models may be either executable or non-executable. The biggest difference between the two is that in executable models, *variables* are explicitly defined in the model, most often by technical users, i.e., programmers. These variables, along with expressions that reference them, allow the logic to be executed on an automation engine. In non-executable models, typically created by business users, variables are often omitted. As a result, the detailed case or process logic may not be fully defined, and certainly not revealed by the printed diagrams. To address this, Method and Style provides conventions that use diagram elements to *imply* the existence of certain variables and expressions without the modeler having to create them explicitly.

In BPMN Method and Style, for example, each end event of a subprocess defines a distinct *end state*, meaning how did the subprocess end, successfully or in some exception state. The end event label names the end state, typically in the form Noun-Adjective, or just Adjective. A subprocess with multiple end states is followed by a gateway with one gate per end state, directing the flow to a different next step based on how the subprocess ended. A BPMN task also may have multiple end states, but you cannot look inside it to see them. Instead, they are

---

implied by the labels of the gates immediately following the task. Two gates, "Approved" and "Rejected", *implies* those values as the task's end states.

These end states implied by gateway and end event labels clarify details of the flow logic in non-executable models. Of course, executable models require explicitly defined variables and gateway logic that explicitly operates on them. In BPMN, variables are called *data objects*, but are almost never defined in non-executable models.

In an ideal world, it would be nice to see BPMN tools *automatically* create those data objects and gateway expressions based simply on the end event and gate labels in the diagram.

CMMN is a little different from BPMN in that (a) it is more likely to be intended for execution, and (b) variables, called *case file items*, are more often created by non-programmers, i.e., business users. The latter is certainly true for documents driving the case logic, but not necessarily for data, including built-in data like milestones and case task end states. For that reason, CMMN Method and Style *implies* the existence of file items to capture that information, even when not explicitly defined by the modeler. In non-executable models, these *implicit file items*, just like explicitly defined file items, may be referenced in conditional logic controlling the case plan, including sentry IF-parts, the rules governing discretionary items, repetition, or manual vs automatic activation.

Once again, in an ideal world, it would be nice to see CMMN tools *automatically* create those file items and conditional logic based simply on certain elements and labels in the diagram.

In CMMN Method and Style, we are concerned in particular with *milestones* and *task end states*.

Milestones

In the CMMN spec, milestones are a type of event. When a milestone is achieved, its *occur* event can trigger sentry ON-parts in the same stage. But in addition, Method and Style persists a list of all *Completed* milestones in an implicit variable *Milestones* variable. Each milestone in the list is represented by the string value *[stage].[milestone]*, which must be unique in the case. The modeler does not need to create this file item; it is defined and updated implicitly.[12] Sentry IF-part expressions can test whether a particular milestone is contained in this list.

Task End States

The benefit of task end states in CMMN is the same as in BPMN: Often the elements enabled to start on completion or exit of a task depend on *how* it ended, successfully or not: its end state. Just like BPMN tasks, CMMN tasks are atomic, so you cannot look inside them to see their end state. Recall that in BPMN Method and Style, task end states are implied by the gate labels of an XOR gateway immediately following the task. Similarly, in CMMN Method and Style, task end states are implied by sentry labels.

---

[12] This is easy to say for non-executable models. Execution of models with such implicit file items requires implementation by the tool vendor.

Here is how that works. As in BPMN Method and Style, CMMN task end states are *exclusive*, meaning a task may have only one end state value, a string. CMMN Method and Style defines an implicit file item *[task].end* holding the end state value. The list of task end states is found by examining all sentry IF-parts referencing values of *[task].end*.[13]

More Flexible Case Logic

Because file items are *global* – visible in any stage of the case – using them to persist the state of milestones and task end states makes the case plan logic even more flexible and powerful. For example, while ON-part links may be triggered only by plan item events in the same stage, they may be triggered by file item *update* events anywhere in the case. This is true even without Method and Style, but adding implicit milestone and task end event file items allows this power to be used more easily and revealed from the printed diagrams.

Sentry Labeling

In Method and Style, a sentry's IF-part condition, a Boolean expression of file item values, is visualized via the *sentry label*. That expression, which could be long and complex, depends on the tool's expression language. In FEEL, however, it most often takes the simple form

```
[file item] = [value]14
```

With implicit file items, in many cases we can simplify the sentry label further. For example, when the ON-part link from a *task* specifies its *complete* or *exit* event and the IF-part tests its end state, we simply label the sentry with the end state value. Thus in this case the sentry label

```
[value]
```

is equivalent to the IF-part condition

```
[task].end = [value]
```

Similarly, when the ON-part link from a *stage* specifies its *complete* or exit *event* and the IF-part tests whether a milestone of the stage has occurred, we simply label the sentry with the milestone name. Thus in this case the sentry label

```
[milestone]
```

is equivalent to the FEEL expression

```
list contains(Milestones, "[stage].[milestone]")
```

---

[13] If the task has non-exclusive end states – more than one could be set at the same time – the modeler must create an explicit file item for the list.

[14] In the FEEL syntax used in this book, = is a comparison operator, not assignment. CMMN tools using a different expression language may have a different IF-part syntax.

In cases where the sentry's ON-part trigger is not a *complete* or *exit* event of a plan item in the stage, the sentry label is the full condition expression, such as

```
[task].end = [value], or
list contains(Milestones, "[stage].[milestone]")
```

CHAPTER 4

Modeling Case Logic

At this point you've seen all the elements used to compose case logic in the plan model. Now let's see how to do it.

A CMMN case is typically much larger than a single BPMN process. It lasts longer and has more steps. Its scope often encompasses multiple processes. A BPMN process typically is the fulfillment of a single request. Each instance of the process has a well-defined start and end. It proceeds from a single start event via predefined sequential logic to one of multiple enumerated end states. The case as a whole, in contrast, does not work like that. There may be multiple ways to start it, and its end state is typically complex. In fact, a case may remain open forever. Progression of the case at runtime often depends on case worker knowledge and decisions not described by any rule-based logic.

Stage Start and Completion

When a stage becomes *Active*, all its contained plan items with no entry conditions become *Available* and immediately transition either to *Enabled* or *Active*, depending on whether or not they are *Manually Activated*. Contained plan items with entry conditions immediately become *Available* and, once their entry condition is satisfied, similarly transition to either *Enabled* or *Active*.

Completion of a stage – either in the *Completed* or *Terminated* state – is a key driver of case logic. If marked *Autocomplete*, the stage becomes *Completed* automatically when no enclosed plan items are *Active* and all *Required* plan items are either *Completed* or *Terminated*. If not *Autocomplete*, a case worker may *manually* move a stage to *Completed* under the same conditions as *Autocomplete*.

A stage moves to *Terminated* automatically when one of its *exit* conditions (black sentry) is satisfied. In addition, an *Active* stage may be moved *manually* to *Terminated* (*terminate* event) by a case worker. Technically, *exit* and *terminate* are distinct standard events.

When a stage becomes either *Completed* or *Terminated*, all its contained plan items that are not themselves *Completed* or *Terminated* are immediately ended.

Using CMMN and BPMN Together

In practice, CMMN and BPMN are best used together. Typically we use CMMN to describe the high-level end-to-end logic, with *process tasks* to invoke BPMN processes contained in the case. Case management vendors like Trisotech and Flowable provide tight integration of BPMN and CMMN in their tools and runtime, making this much easier.

Even where most of the logic is procedural, meaning individual pieces of the case are easily described in BPMN, the overall behavior may be better modeled in CMMN. As an example of this, Flowable suggests the CMMN model shown in Figure 25. The logic is simple but not easily replicated in BPMN.

The scenario is managing the lifecycle of a client account. When the case starts – how a case starts is not shown in CMMN – the process task *Initialize Client User* becomes immediately *Active*, invoking a BPMN process. The two stages *Manage Active User* and *Manage Inactive User* have entry conditions, so they are *Available* but not yet *Active* when the case starts. At the same time, the process task *Delete user* is immediately *Enabled*, awaiting manual activation before becoming *Active*.

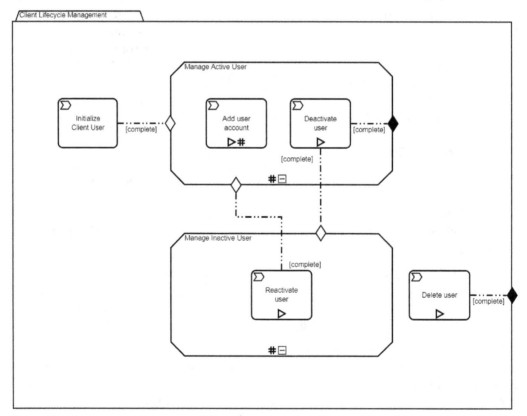

Figure 25. Stages as case states enabling process tasks. Source: Flowable

When the process *Initialize Client User* is complete, the stage *Manage Active User* transitions from *Available* to *Active* and its contained process tasks *Add user account* and *Deactivate user* automatically become *Enabled,* awaiting manual activation. Presumably a case worker would normally activate *Add user account,* another process task, but this is not strictly required by the model. He could instead run *Deactivate user.* When the process *Add user account* completes, the process task returns to the *Enabled* state because it is marked *Repeatable.* This allows the case worker to add another account for the user. The case remains in this state until a case worker starts *Deactivate user,* another process task. When the associated BPMN process completes, two sentries are triggered. The stage *Manage Active User* becomes *Terminated* and the stage *Manage Inactive User* becomes *Active.*

Activation of *Manage Inactive User* moves its plan item *Reactivate user* to *Enabled.* When run by a case worker the reactivation process is invoked, and when it completes, again two things happen: First, the stage *Manage Inactive User* automatically transitions to the *Completed* state. Second, the stage *Manage Active User* is triggered again, becoming *Active.*

At any time during the case, a case worker may run *Delete user.* When its associated process completes, the case moves to *Terminated.* The behavior described by this CMMN diagram is difficult to model in BPMN.

Style Rule Consistency

However, as drawn in Figure 25, this model violates the style rule forbidding links that cross stage boundaries. Instead, Method and Style asks you to draw it as shown in Figure 26. Now activation of a stage is not triggered by a plan item contained in another stage but by an event of the other stage itself, so there are no links crossing stage boundaries. In Figure 25, the *complete* event of *Deactivate User* triggers both the exit condtion of *Manage Active User* and the entry condition of *Manage Inactive User.* In Figure 26, it directly triggers only the exit of *Manage Active User,* and the *exit* event of that stage is what triggers the entry of *Manage Inactive User.*

Note that in stage *Manage Active User,* with both process tasks in the *Enabled* state, a case worker *could* manually declare the stage *Completed.* Perhaps that was not the modeler's intent, but it is allowed by the diagram as described above. That is why *complete* was added as a second event on the link to the entry of *Manage Inactive User.*[15] Without that, the case could be left in a *zombie state*: *Manage Active User* is *Completed, Manage Inactive User* is *Available,* so neither stage is *Active,* with no path of recovery except *Delete user.*

---

[15] Note: A comma-separated list of standard events on the link label is a Triostech extension. Technically the spec requires two separate entry conditions, one for each event. The Trisotech extension is just a graphical one; in the XML interchange format each event is a separate entry condition.

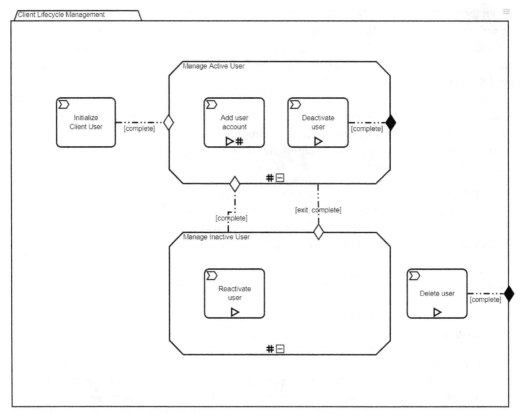

Figure 26. Corrected diagram of stages as case states enabling process tasks

Avoiding Zombie States

A zombie state is the CMMN equivalent to a deadlocked join in BPMN. The instance is stuck with no way forward or back, and this pattern is typically not detected by model validation. Without the addition of the complete link from *Manage Active User* in Figure 26, a zombie state would be created if *Manage Active User* was manually marked *Completed*, even though the modeler may not have anticipated that possibility. Zombie states can arise when the modeler expects one stage to be *Active* at any time but does not account for both *complete* and *exit* transitions from all stages. Adding the *complete* event to the expected *exit* link is one way to fix the problem.

An alternative fix would be to mark *Deactivate user* as *Required*, preventing a case worker from manually declaring *Active* to be *Completed*. In that case, the stage *Manage Active User* could never become *Completed*, only *Terminated*.

Manual Termination

One plan item lifecycle event we do not discuss much in this book is *terminate*, meaning manual termination of an *Active* task or stage. In theory, this could happen in any task or stage at any time for any reason, but in practice I suspect this operation will often be unavailable in the runtime user interface, except perhaps for special administrator roles, and for good reason. Even though both *exit* and *terminate* transition to the same *Terminated* state, they are distinct events, and accounting for the possibility of *terminate* on every task or stage could lead to a clutter of seldom-used ON-part links. I put *terminate* in the same category as *suspend* and *fault*, events related to runtime exceptions that normally have no place in descriptive (non-executable) case models.

It is important to remember that *terminate* of a plan item could cause its containing stage to become *Completed*, which may not be the modeler's intent. If you plan to allow *terminate* in your CMMN models, I recommend linking the terminating plan item to a *milestone* that triggers *exit* of the containing stage. This will allow more orderly handling of the exception.

Method and Style: Task and Stage End States

As discussed in Chapter 3, in order to reveal the logic as clearly as possible from the printed diagrams, Method and Style assumes various conventions that are not part of the CMMN standard, such as *end states* of tasks and stages persisted for use in the case logic.

Task End States

As discussed previously, Method and Style assumes that every task *implicitly* generates a file item *[taskname].end* with enumerated text values naming each *end state*. The end state, typically in the form Noun-Adjective, is normally a single string describing *how* the task ended, successfully or in some exception state. Moreover, a task's end states are normally *exclusive*, meaning only a single value is allowed. If the task end state is not a single string value, such as a list or structure, the modeler is required to *explicitly* define a file item of the appropriate type, such as *[taskname].endObject*, to hold the value.

The end state value may be tested by sentry IF-parts. If the ON-part of that sentry is the task's *complete* or *exit* event, labeling the sentry with the end state [value] is a visual shortcut meaning the FEEL expression

```
[taskname].end = [value]
```

If the sentry's ON-part links to some other plan item or standard event, the sentry label should be the full FEEL expression.

Method and Style further assumes that in the case of a *process task*, *[taskname].end* holds the name of the BPMN process end event reached, assuming only one. If the process instance reaches more than one – strongly discouraged in BPMN Method and Style, but possible – the modeler is required to *explicitly* define a file item such as *[taskname].endObject* to hold the end event names. In this case, any IF-parts referencing such an end state should be labeled with the full FEEL expression.

In the case of a *decision task*, the end state is the output value of the DMN decision model, which is normally a simple value but possibly a structure or list. Similarly, if the decision output is not a single simple value and other case logic depends on the end state value, the modeler must explicitly create a file item *[taskname].endObject* to hold the value.

Stage End States

For stages, Method and Style uses milestones to represent end states and intermediate states. It assumes that each milestone in the *Completed* state is automatically contained in the *implicit* file item *Milestones,* a string list, with the value *[stagename].[milestone].* This file item may be tested by sentry IF-parts, and if the ON-part of that sentry is the stage's *complete* or *exit* event, labeling the sentry as `[milestone]` corresponds to the FEEL expression

```
list contains(Milestones, "[stagename].[milestone]")
```

If the ON-part links to a different plan item or standard event, the IF-part label `[stagename].[milestone]` is used. This mechanism provides a way to reveal common flow patterns via simple sentry labels.

Example

Here is an example. The scenario is registration of a client for social care. The case starts on receipt of a Support request, which activates the first stage, *Registration* (Figure 27).

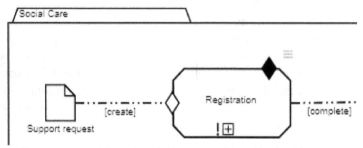

Figure 27. Fragment of top-level diagram with collapsed *Registration* stage

You could argue that *Registration* is really a process and should be modeled as a process task, but to illustrate the use of task end states and milestones, we model it as a stage.

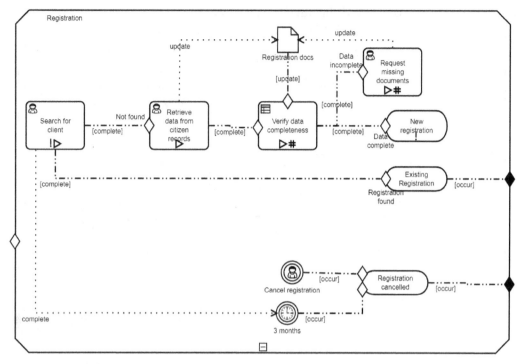

Figure 28. Child page expansion of *Registration* stage, one *Completed* end state, two *Terminated* end states

The child page expanded view of the stage is shown in Figure 28. It starts by searching the registration database for the client. From the diagram we see that the task *Search for client* has two end states, "Registration found" and "Not found". We can tell that because those are the labels of sentries triggered by the task's *complete* event. Method and Style thus assumes the implicit file item *Search for client.end* has enumerated values "Registration found" and "Not found".

If an existing registration is found, the milestone *Existing registration* is triggered and the stage *exits*. If no existing registration is found, data about the client is retrieved from citizen records and verified for completeness using a decision task. The decision output values are either "Data complete" or "Data incomplete", again implied by sentry labels. If information is incomplete, missing documents are requested, and that cycle repeats until the registration data is complete, at which point the milestone *New registration* is triggered. If a new registration is not completed within 3 months of the initial search, the milestone *Registration cancelled* is triggered and the stage *exits*. A case worker also may cancel registration at any time.

We see this stage has three milestones, which we can interpret as end states of the stage. Unlike BPMN Method and Style, where subprocess end states are normally exclusive – only one is reached in any instance – CMMN Method and Style milestones do not have that constraint. Here we see that two of the milestones represent *exit* states and one, *New registration*, represents *complete*. The milestone *New registration* is marked *Required*, meaning the stage cannot *complete* unless this milestone is achieved. In order to avoid zombie states, it is always good practice for a stage to have a single *Required* milestone representing *complete*. Here's why.

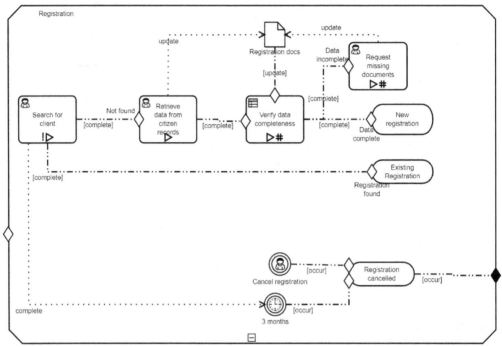

Figure 29. Multiple non-exit milestones with no *Required* milestone allows zombie states.

Let's say we did not mark *New Registration* as *Required* and we considered *Existing registration* a second *complete* end state, i.e., removing the link to *exit* (Figure 29). In that case, a user could manually mark the stage *Completed* as long as no task is *Active*, but without reaching any of the milestones. If the modeler assumed that the next stage after *complete* depends on one of the milestones always being set, the case would be deadlocked in a zombie state. By making *Existing registration* an *exit* end state and marking *New registration* as *Required* eliminates this possibility.

In general, you can avoid these zombie states by having a single *Required* non-*exit* milestone in a stage, plus any number of *exit* end states. Sometimes, however, you may want to model a stage with more than one non-*exit* end state. You can still do that safely by adding an extra *Required* milestone, triggered by the non-*exit* end state milestones.

For example, in Figure 30, achieving either *New registration* or *Existing registration* triggers the milestone *Registration complete,* which is marked *Required.* Now a case worker now may not manually complete the stage unless either *New registration* or *Existing registration* has been set. The *complete* event of *Registration* now could mean either a new registration or an existing one.

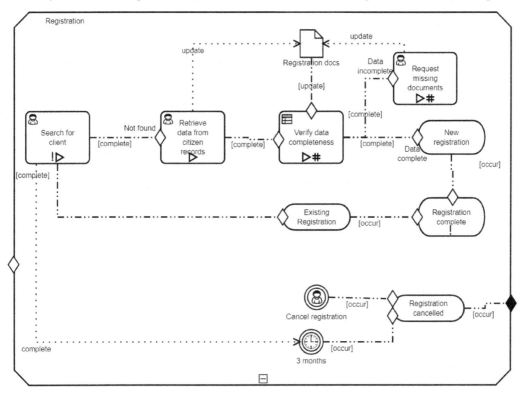

Figure 30. Alternative child page expansion of *Registration*, two *Completed* end states, one *Terminated* end state.

If the subsequent case logic depends on which of these milestones was achieved, the link to the stage's *complete* event simply specifies the name of the milestone in the sentry label.

For example (Figure 31), stage *Acceptance* is triggered when *Registration* is *complete* if milestone *New registration* was achieved. The sentry label "New registration" is shorthand for the IF-part FEEL expression

```
list contains(Milestones, "Registration.New registration")
```

where *Milestones* is the implicit file item used to list all case milestones in the *Completed* state.

Similarly, stage *Preventive Counseling* is triggered either when *Registration* is *complete* and milestone *Existing registration* was achieved, or *Registration* is *exit*.

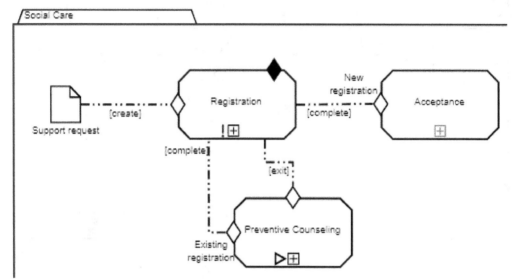

Figure 31. Branch on stage end state

Stages as Exclusive Case States

One useful way to model end-to-end case logic is hierarchically using collapsed stages in the top-level diagram representing *exclusive case states*. The logic shown in Figure 32 illustrates one way to do this.

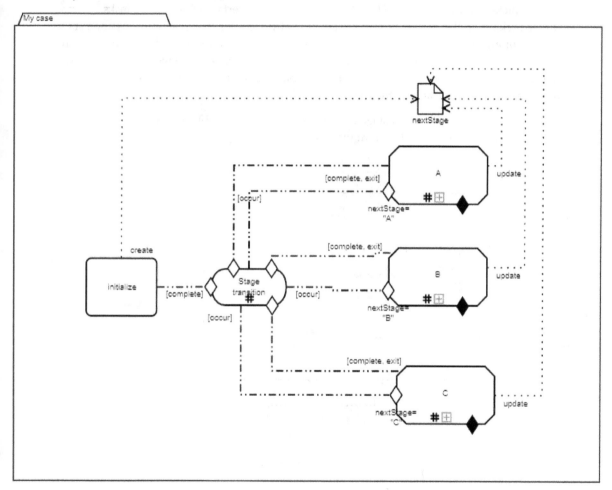

Figure 32. Stages *A*, *B*, and *C* are exclusive case states, only one *Active* at a time

When the case starts, the *initialize* task *creates* the file item *nextStage* and populates it with the name of the next stage to become *Active*. When *initialize* completes, the milestone *Stage transition* is activated. The *occur* event of *Stage transition* is broadcast to all stages in the case. The entry criterion IF-part of each stage looks for its own stage name in the file item value. This ensures that only one stage is activated. The *Active* stage updates the file item *nextStage* prior to *complete* or *exit*, either of which triggers the milestone and the cycle continues.

This use of CMMN as a flexible top-level state machine is useful even if the stages contain primarily (or only) process tasks.

Plan Items as UI Elements

Although CMMN does not specify how case information is presented to case workers at runtime, it is natural to think of the set of plan items that are currently either *Enabled* awaiting manual activation, awaiting a user event listener, or discretionary and "plannable" as buttons or menu picks in the case runtime UI, along with the user interface of any *Active* tasks.. A case worker clicking on the button or menu pick manually activates that plan item. As one stage *completes* or *exits* and another one *starts*, the set of buttons/menu picks changes automatically. And don't forget, stages may contain other stages, and, like tasks, stages may be marked *Manually Activated*, so the menu of currently available case worker actions can be quite dynamic and generated automatically by the CMMN model.

For example, in Figure 33, when stage *Acceptance* starts, the available user actions are exposed in a toolbar (Figure 34) generated from the case plan.

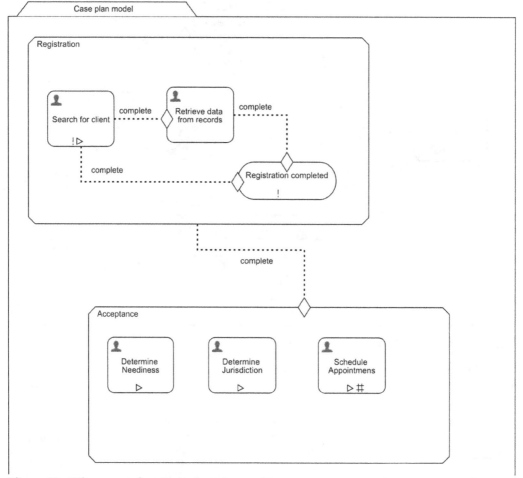

Figure 33. When case plan starts *Acceptance* stage...

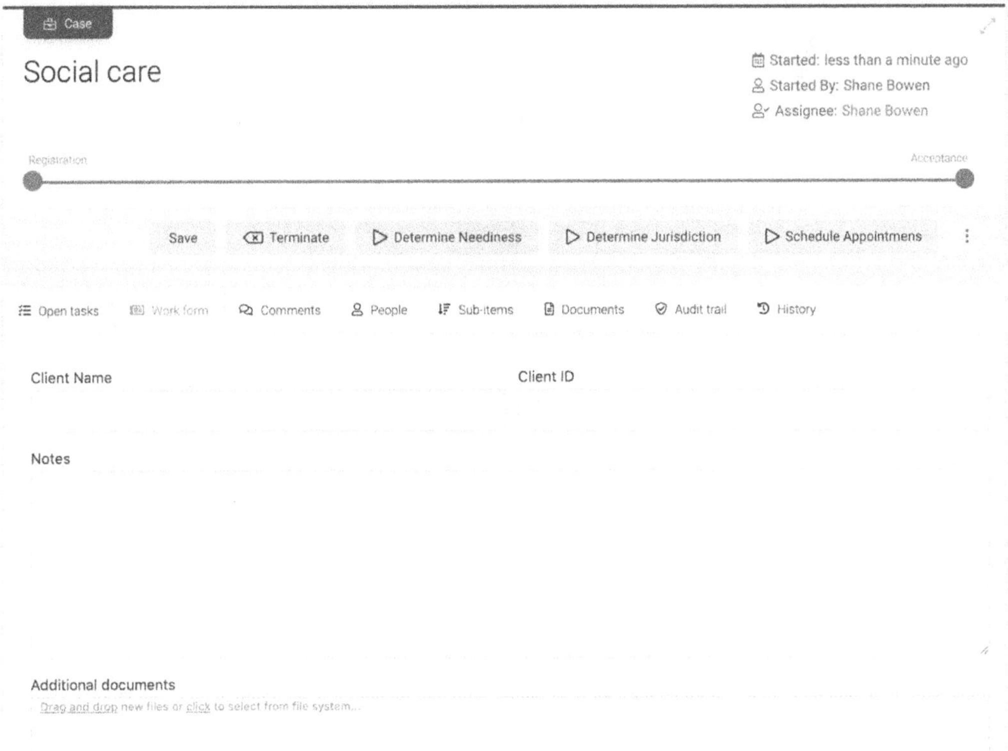

Figure 34. …the user interface provides a toolbar of available actions. Source: Flowable

Thinking about stages in this way helps you organize the structure of the case model. One tool vendor, FICO, has even formalized this approach in a methodology called xDRAW.[16]

---

[16] https://slideplayer.com/slide/14292614/

CHAPTER 5

Styles of Case Modeling

When creating case models in CMMN, there is no single "best" style for representing the logic. Some modelers may consider progression of the case to be entirely based on the judgment of case workers rather than events and rules specified at design time. In that style, what happens in what order is not revealed by the diagram. The case worker is simply assumed to know the correct thing to do next, even though this permits illogical ordering of tasks.

Others may take the opposite point of view, describing most case logic explicitly *using event-condition-action* (ECA) via lifecycle events and sentries. While intrinsically more flexible than BPMN, CMMN models in this style are similar in that in principle they can reveal all possibilities of "what happens next" through the diagram.

Still others may see CMMN's role primarily as controlling the current *state* of the case – modeled as the currently *Active* stage – with each stage containing primarily process and decision tasks modeled in BPMN and DMN. A variant of this style uses the currently *Active* stage as a way to populate a menu or toolbar of available next actions, each represented by a UI fragment.

All of these perspectives are equally legitimate. In fact, a single case model often will contain elements of all three.

Scenario: Write a Report

In this chapter, we'll simply illustrate the similarities and differences when applied to a very simple scenario, writing a report. Its steps are as follows:

1. The report may or may not require research. If it does, tasks include researching the topic and organizing references.

2. Preparing the draft is always required. It includes writing the text, also always required, and generating the table of contents. If the report contains graphics, additional tasks include creating the graphics, integrating them with the text, and generating a list of figures.

3. Periodically the draft in progress is reviewed. Tasks include seeking comments, discussing possible changes, and verifying spelling and grammar.

4. When ready, the draft is submitted for approval. The case completes successfully when the report is approved. It is also possible that the Approver cancels the report.

User-Driven Style

In the purest user-driven style, all choices of what to do when are made by case workers at runtime using their judgment about what needs to happen, as illustrated in Figure 35.

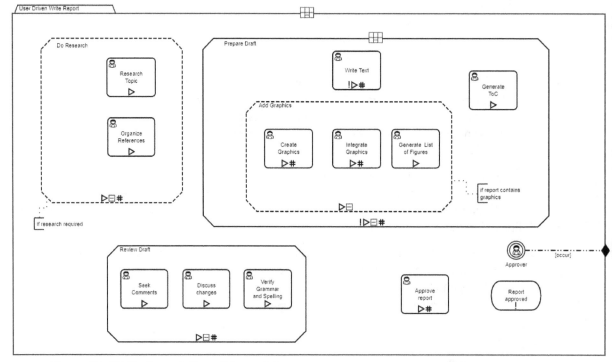

Figure 35. Write Report, User-driven style

The stage *Do Research* is discretionary, meaning it occurs in some instances and not in others. In the diagram here there is an *applicability rule*, defined in the planning table shown on the case boundary and visualized in the diagram as a *text annotation* on the stage. Alternatively, there might be no applicability rule, just an authorized role specified in the planning table. If research is required, this stage transitions to *Enabled* when directed via the planning table, awaiting manual start by a case worker. When it starts (becomes *Active*), its tasks *Research Topic* and *Organize References* become *Enabled*, awaiting manual start. As drawn here, whether this stage ends in *Completed* or *Terminated* does not affect case completion.

Since it has no entry condition, the stage *Prepare Draft* is *Enabled* as soon as the case becomes *Active*. Since it is marked *Required*, the case cannot complete until this stage is *Completed* or *Terminated*, and the stage cannot *complete* until its *Required* task *Write Text* is *Completed* or

Terminated. Other than that, the order in which its contained plan items are performed is determined entirely by the case worker.

The contained stage *Add Graphics* is discretionary, as it applies only to reports that contain graphics. Again, the applicability rule is defined in a planning table, here on the containing stage *Prepare Draft*, and visualized in the diagram by a text annotation on the discretionary stage. If the applicability rule is true, *Add Graphics* is *Enabled* when *Prepare Draft* becomes *Active* and must be manually started by a case worker. Its tasks include *Create Graphics, Integrate Graphics,* and *Generate List of Figures*.

Prepare Draft also includes the task *Generate ToC,* which could be considered "optional" since it is not marked *Required*. In practice there is little difference between such an optional task and a non-*Required* discretionary task.

The case also contains the task *Approve report*. It is not enclosed in a stage, meaning it becomes *Enabled* as soon as the case is *Active*. Presumably it would not be started until a draft of the report was complete or nearly so, but this is not required by the case plan model.

The milestone *Report Approved* is marked *Required*, meaning the case can end in the *Completed* state only if this milestone is set manually by a case worker. Alternatively, a case worker in the role *Approver* may terminate the case at any time, depicted as a *user event listener* triggering an *exit* sentry. As mentioned previously, using *exit* is recommended over the *terminate* event.

In Figure 35, all the stages and many tasks are marked *Repeatable*. Since no entry conditions are specified, that means that after being marked *Completed* or *Terminated* a plan item immediately becomes *Enabled* again. The effect of *Repeatable* here is simply protection against a case worker mistakenly completing or terminating a task or stage. Technically, this creates a new instance of the plan item, as CMMN has no way to "reopen" a completed or terminated plan item, but we assume the artifacts created by the original instance are available as file items to the new instance.

ECA Style

The ECA style, in contrast, represents the allowed order of plan items explicitly as much as possible using lifecycle transitions and sentries. It allows for a great deal more automated behavior than does the user-driven style, but at the same time the notation may be more difficult for stakeholders on the business side to understand.

The same scenario is illustrated in ECA style in Figure 36. Here the possible ordering of case actions is explicit. Because it is the plan item's *complete* event that usually triggers what happens next, this case could probably be modeled more simply and clearly as a BPMN process. Let's take a closer look.

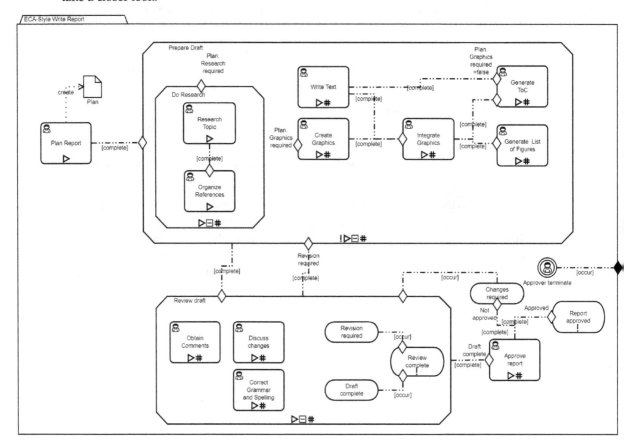

Figure 36. Write Report, ECA style

When the case first starts, the only plan item enabled is *Plan Report*, which creates the file item *Plan*. We need something like this to say that *Do Research* and *Create Graphics* are only performed under certain conditions, expressed as components of the file item *Plan*.

When *Plan Report* completes, the *Required* stage *Prepare Draft* is *Enabled*. When the stage becomes *Active*, task *Write Text* is always *Enabled*; stage *Do Research* is *Enabled* if *Plan.Research required* is true; and task *Create Graphics* is *Enabled* if *Plan.Graphics required* is true.

The task *Integrate Graphics* is *Enabled* when both *Write Text* and *Create Graphics* are *Completed*. If *Create Graphics* is not performed, then *Integrate Graphics* and *Generate List of Figures* will not be performed, either, as they depend on completion of *Create Graphics*. The task *Generate ToC* is *Enabled* either when *Write Text* is *Completed* and there are no graphics, or when *Integrate Graphics* is *Completed*.

None of the plan items of *Prepare Draft* are *Required*, meaning the stage may be declared *Completed* whenever none of its plan items are *Active*. This triggers the stage *Review draft*, which contains tasks *Obtain comments, Discuss changes,* and *Correct Grammar and Spelling*, performed in parallel. We'd like to say that *Review draft* has two manually set end state milestones, either *Draft complete* or *Revision required*, but, as previously discussed, in order to prevent a zombie state in which the stage is declared *Completed* without setting either milestone, we also need to add the *Required* milestone *Review Complete*, which depends on achieving one of those two end states.

If *Review draft* completes in the *Revision required* end state, the *Repeatable* stage *Prepare draft* is triggered again. As discussed in Chapter 4, the sentry IF-part label "Revision required" is shorthand for the FEEL expression

```
list contains(Milestones, "Review draft.Revision required")
```

where *Milestones* is the implicit file item used to hold the list of completed milestones. Since the ON-part link is from *Review draft*, we may omit that prefix from the sentry label. Similarly, if *Review draft* completes in the *Review Complete* end state, we go on to *Approve report*.

Approve report has task end states "Approved" and "Not approved", which are tested by sentry IF-parts to trigger either the milestone *Report approved* or the milestone *Changes required*. The sentry label "Approved" is shorthand for the FEEL expression

```
Approve report.end="Approved"
```

The milestone *Report approved* acts as an end state of the case as a whole; the case can end in the *Completed* state only when *Report approved* is set. The milestone *Changes required* retriggers *Review draft* and then likely back to *Prepare draft* for revision.

As in the user-driven model, an Approver also can terminate the case at any time.

Hierarchical Style

It could be overkill for such simple case logic, but we can also model this scenario as a tree or hierarchy of diagrams, with all stages in the top level rendered as collapsed, each expanded in a separate child-level diagram. This style not only allows very large and complex case logic to be captured on diagrams that each fit on a single page, but best supports the notion of the case as a high-level state machine, with a stage corresponding to each case state. The internal logic of each stage can be modeled in a style appropriate to its logic: user-driven, ECA, or possibly simply a collection of process tasks.

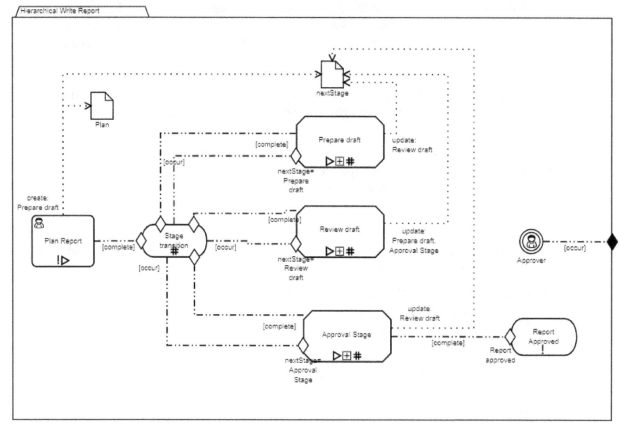

Figure 37. Hierarchical Write Report – top level

In the top-level diagram (Figure 37), all stages are collapsed. This diagram illustrates the pattern described previously in which only one stage, representing a state of the case, is *Active* at a time. It is implemented via a file item *nextStage* that is updated by each stage just prior to completing. The stage *complete* event triggers the *Repeatable* milestone *Stage transition*, which in turn is linked to all stages in the case. The IF-part of that link selects the stage named by the file item.

This mechanism allows the case state to freely bounce back and forth between the stages *Prepare draft, Review draft,* and *Approval Stage,* something more difficult to achieve in BPMN.

The case starts with the task *Plan Report,* also described previously, which creates the file item *Plan,* used to determine whether research and/or graphics are required. The case is *complete* when the *Required* milestone *Report Approved* is set. Alternatively, an Approver may *exit* the case at any time.

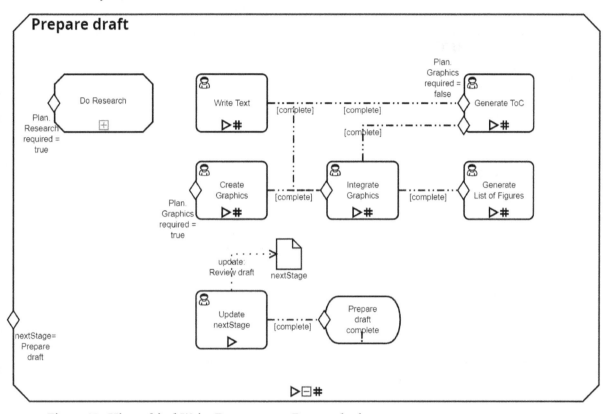

Figure 38. Hierarchical Write Report, stage *Prepare draft*

Figure 38 shows the child-level expansion of *Prepare draft.* In this representation, the control symbols at bottom center must match the collapsed shape in the parent, and the sentry IF-part labels on the boundary must match as well. Links to sentries from outside the stage are not displayed in the child diagram.

The child diagram may contain other collapsed stages, as you see here with *Do Research,* which would be detailed in a grandchild-level diagram. *Do Research* has an entry condition with no ON-part but an IF-part. No ON-part means the IF-part is evaluated when the containing stage, *Prepare Draft,* becomes *Active.* Since *Prepare draft* is *Manually Activated,* that means after *manual start* by a case worker. As discussed in the ECA style model, the IF-part tests the file item *Plan* to determine whether research is required.

Similarly, the task *Create Graphics* is *Enabled* when *Prepare draft* becomes *Active* if the file item *Plan* indicates graphics are required in the report.

The tasks *Write Text* and *Update nextStage* become *Enabled* unconditionally when *Prepare draft* becomes *Active*. Even though it might not make sense to do so, *Update nextStage* may be performed at any time, even before *Write Text* is *Completed*. As long as no contained plan item is *Active* and the *Required* milestone *Prepare draft complete* is set, this stage may be declared *Completed*. This ensures that the file item *nextStage* has been updated.

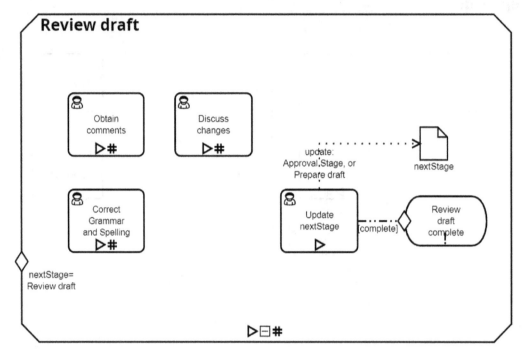

Figure 39. Hierarchical Write Report, stage *Review draft*

Figure 39 depicts the child-page expansion of *Review draft*. It uses the user-driven style, in which all tasks are enabled when the stage becomes *Active*. What to do at any time is determined by manual case worker action. You can also envision how these tasks could be represented by menu picks or toolbar icons in the case runtime user interface, each selecting a UI fragment appropriate to the selected task.

Unlike *Prepare draft*, here there is a choice of *nextStage* value, either *Approval Stage* if no revisions are required or *Prepare draft* if further changes are needed. This selection is made manually by a case worker. This stage may be declared *Completed* when no task is *Active* and the *Required* milestone *Review draft complete* is set.

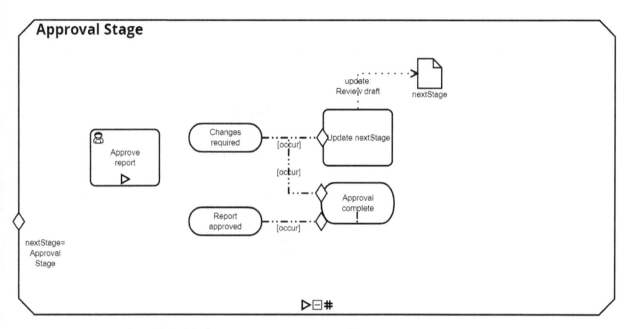

Figure 40. Hierarchical Write Report, stage *Approval Stage*

Figure 40 depicts the child page expansion of *Approval Stage*. The only real action here is the task *Approve report*. This stage has end states *Changes required* or *Report approved*, represented by manually set milestones, either of which sets the *Required* milestone *Approval complete*. In addition, if *Changes required* is set, the file item *nextStage* is updated. Otherwise, when this stage is *Completed*, the case transitions to the *Required* milestone *Report Approved* in the top-level diagram (Figure 37).

CHAPTER 6

CMMN by Example: Social Care

In this chapter we will illustrate use of CMMN Method and Style with an example based on Social Care in a European country, adapted from a client-provided scenario.

Scenario

All citizens who meet certain jurisdictional and need requirements are entitled to Social Care from the government. Benefits include both material care – direct client payments, payment to healthcare providers, housing, etc. – and personal care benefits such as counseling and training. In addition, preventive counseling benefits are offered to those who fail to meet all the Social Care acceptance requirements.

The Social Care client is an individual or family requesting Social Care support. Each client represents an instance of the case. The case starts on receipt of the first support request from the client. If registration does not find the client in the system, the client must be registered, based on identity check, verification of income, bank records and the like. Successful registration continues to acceptance, which verifies the client is eligible for Social Care.

If registration detects the client is already involved in an active case, there is no need to recheck eligibility. The new support request is simply added to the active case. If registration detects the client is registered but in a stored file, meaning a closed case, an active case is reopened for the client.

If either registration or acceptance is not successful, or if the active case is terminated for some reason, the applicant is directed to preventive counseling, a set of services outside of the normal Social Care system.

Once in an active case, the client is assigned a social worker and a clerk. The social worker may assign a set of functions to the clerk, a process called delegation, which is reviewed on a biweekly basis. Based on periodic assessment, the client is assigned to one of four segments – A, B, C, or D. Segmentation may also decide to close the active case. After a delay to cover any outstanding invoices, a closed active case moves to a stored file.

During an active case, all conversations, inquiries, clarifications, and the like are memorialized in writing within the case file.

In the stored file state, the complete case file is archived in a document management system with retention management features, including the ability to apply a legal hold on the information. It is still possible for case workers to consult the stored file if needed. If a new support request is received from the client in the stored file state, an active case is reopened.

If the case remains in the stored file state for ten years, it is moved to the state archive and the case instance is terminated.

Case Model Structure

Initially my *Social Care* case model included stages *Registration, Acceptance, Active Case,* and *Stored File,* but I realized that this would not work. Each instance of the case pertains to a separate registered client, but at the start of *Registration* – triggered by an incoming support request – whether the requester is a new or existing client is unknown.

That means that *Registration* cannot be a part of this case! While issues of instance alignment – critical in BPMN – arise less frequently in CMMN, you cannot ignore the case instance entirely. If you want each instance of the *Social Care* case model to mean a particular client, you need a separate case or process to deal with incoming support requests from unknown individuals.

I changed my case model to two interacting cases: *Intake,* in which the instance is a received support request, and *Social Care,* in which the instance is a registered client. *Intake* contains the stages *Registration, Acceptance,* and *Preventive Counseling. Social Care* contains only the stages *Active Case* and *Stored File.*

For new clients, *Intake* includes a non-blocking case task that calls *Social Care,* creating a new instance of that case model but not waiting for it to complete. (For existing clients, an instance of *Social Care* already exists.) Whether a new or existing client, *Intake* ends by creating the file item *Social care update,* which passes details of the *Support request* and registration information to the *Social Care* instance.

Intake

Figure 41 shows the top-level case plan model for *Intake,* drawn in the hierarchical style. An instance of this case is created on receipt of a *Support request,* modeled as a file item *create* event. Unlike a BPMN process, which typically is started by an event, a case in CMMN must be started manually. That means that receipt of *Support request* does not automatically trigger the case. Once the case is started manually, it detects a new file item – modeled as the *create* event of *Support request* – and that triggers the first stage, *Registration.*

There are three *complete* event links plus one *exit* link shown for *Registration,* each representing a different end state of the stage. As discussed in Chapter 4, stage end states are represented by milestones. With a *complete* or *exit* link, the sentry label indicates the end state name. Thus, if *Registration* completes in the state *New registration,* the stage *Acceptance* is started. As explained in Chapter 4, the sentry label "New registration" is visual shorthand for the FEEL IF-part expression

```
list contains(Milestones, "Registration. New registration")
```

where *Milestones* is the implicit file item holding the list of all currently *Completed* case milestones.

When *Acceptance* completes, the non-blocking case task *Social Care* is started, creating a new instance of *Social Care*. As a non-blocking task, it completes immediately, triggering the milestone *New client*.

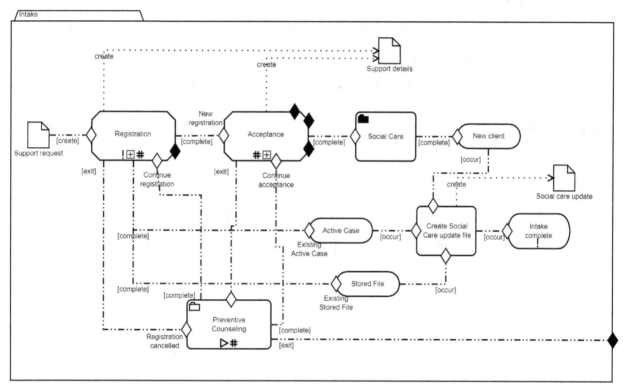

Figure 41. *Intake* case instance is a Social Care support

If *Registration* completes in the state *Existing Active Case*, the milestone *Active Case* is triggered. If it completes in the state *Existing Stored File*, the milestone *Stored File* is triggered. The milestones *New client, Active Case,* and *Stored File* represent alternative end states of the case instance. Any one of them triggers the *Required* milestone *Intake complete*. This ensures that the case may not be completed without achieving one of those three end states.

Just prior to completion of this case, new information captured from the *Support request* and possibly *Registration* and *Acceptance* are used to create the file item *Social care update*. The structure of this model requires that access to the file item is shared by *Intake* and *Social Care*.

Registration also contains one *exit*, meaning it does not complete normally. *Exit* triggers *Preventive Counseling*, modeled as a blocking case task. The details of *Preventive Counseling* are omitted from this model. There are two *complete* links out of *Preventive Counseling*, representing two end states. If the requester is not yet registered, the end state *Continue registration* re-enables the stage *Registration*. If the requester is registered but not yet accepted, the end state *Continue acceptance* re-enables the stage *Acceptance*. The *exit* link from *Preventive Counseling* terminates the case. The *Repeatable* marker is required for *Registration, Acceptance,* and *Preventive Counseling* because each could be triggered more than once.

Registration

Figure 42 shows the child-level expansion of the stage *Registration*. Note that the count of white and black sentries must match between the parent and child-level diagrams, and the IF-part labels should match as well. Only ON-part links from inside the stage are shown in the child diagram; only links from outside the stage are shown in the parent diagram.

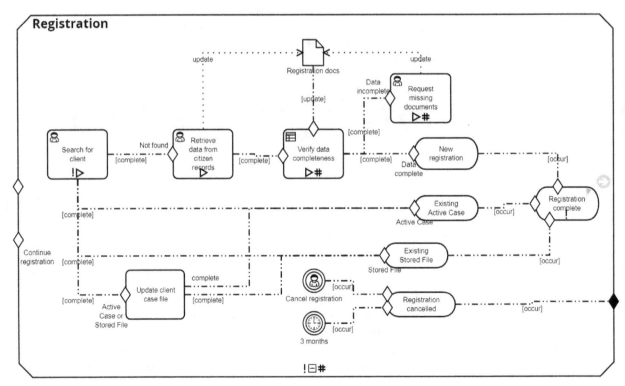

Figure 42. Child page expansion of stage *Registration*

This stage could easily have been modeled as a process task instead, as the steps follow a procedural flow. When the stage starts, the user task *Search for client* is enabled immediately, trying to identify the requester in the Social Care database. As indicated by the sentry labels of the *complete* links from this task, it has end states *Not found, Active Case,* and *Stored File.*

If *Not found,* the task *Retrieve data from citizen records* is enabled, followed by the decision task *Verify data completeness,* with end states *Data complete* and *Data incomplete. Data complete* triggers the end state milestone *New registration. Data incomplete* triggers the task *Request missing documents.* There is no task shown here to *Receive missing documents.* Instead this is represented by the *update* event of the file item *Registration docs,* at which time it retries the *Verify data completeness* decision.

If *Search for client* returns either *Active Case* or *Stored File,* the *Support request* information is used to *update* the client case file, after which the appropriate milestone, *Existing Active Case* or *Existing Stored File,* is triggered immediately. Once again, the *Required* milestone *Registration complete* ensures that this stage may not *complete* unless one of the three end state milestones are achieved.

Registration may *exit* either manually on user cancellation or automatically if the stage does not complete in three months.

Acceptance

Figure 43 shows the child-level expansion of the stage *Acceptance,* which determines eligibility for Social Care. Again, the count and labels of sentries on the boundary must match between parent and child levels.

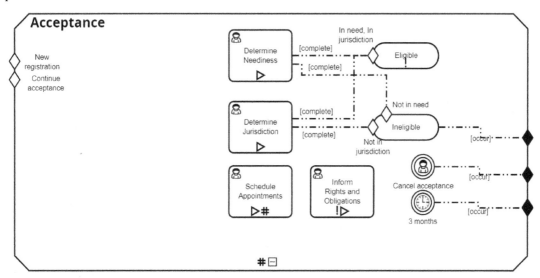

Figure 43. Child page expansion of stage *Acceptance*

Because this stage involves appointments with the requester, the task order is somewhat unpredictable, so the User-driven style is employed in the model. None of the four user tasks have entry conditions, meaning they are all enabled upon start of the stage *Acceptance*, simply awaiting *Manual Activation*.

The *Required* milestone *Eligible* must be triggered in order for this stage to *complete*. That in turn requires *Determine Neediness* to *complete* in end state *In need* and *Determine Jurisdiction* to *complete* in end state *In jurisdiction*. Combining the *complete* links in a single sentry means the entry criteria are ANDed. If either of those tasks *completes* in some other end state, *Acceptance exits*. *Acceptance* may also *exit* automatically if it takes more than three months to *complete* or manually on case worker command.

Social Care

Figure 44 shows the case plan model for *Social Care*, where each instance represents a registered and accepted client. In the hierarchical style, the top-level diagram is quite simple.

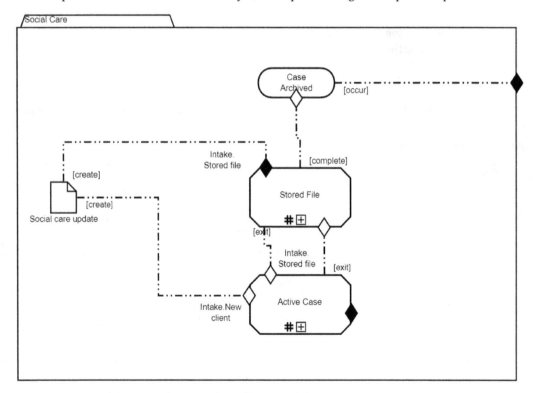

Figure 44. *Social Care* case instance is a client receiving care

From Figure 41, note that a new instance of the case *Social Care* is created by the *Intake* case task *Social Care* for new clients only. For existing clients, an instance of *Social Care* already exists, either in the state *Active Case* or *Stored File*. As seen in Figure 44, for existing clients with an active case, creation of the file item *Social care update* does *not* trigger a new instance of the stage *Active Case*. If *Intake* determines the support request is from a *Stored File* client, in *Social Care* the stage *Stored File* exits and *Active Case* starts.

At any time until the case is archived and *exits*, either stage *Active Case* or *Stored File* is *Active*, never both at the same time. The stage *Active Case* never *completes*; it can only *exit*. The stage *Stored File* only *completes* when it is dormant for ten years, at which time it is archived and the case *exits*. It may *exit* and transition to *Active Case* either on receipt of a new *Support request* or manually on case worker command.

Active Case

Figure 45 shows the child-level expansion of *Active Case*.

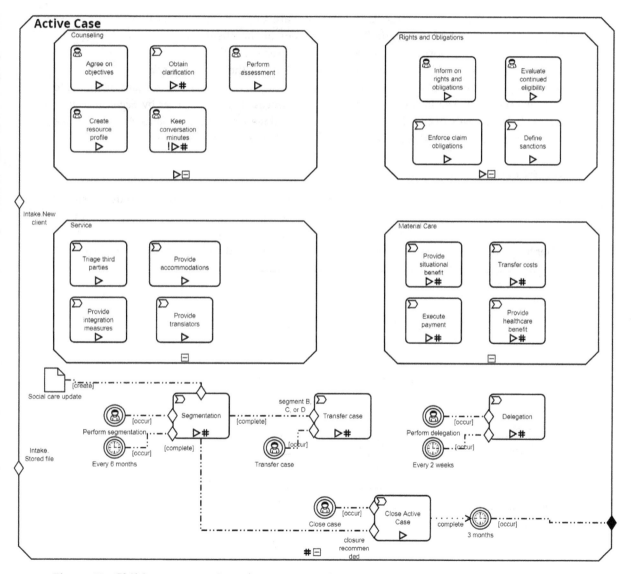

Figure 45. Child page expansion of stage *Active Case*

Most of the activity in *Social Care* occurs in this stage. What happens when is almost entirely enabled manually by case workers, so this is modeled in the User-driven style. All the plan items shown here in the four expanded stages are in the *Enabled* state awaiting *manual start* by a case worker. In that sense they represent menu picks in the runtime user interface. Each of the four expanded stages shown here – *Counseling, Rights and Obligations, Service,* and *Material Care* – is typically delegated to a member of the care team, so it is possible that the case runtime could restrict the menu picks only to the responsible case worker. Most of the activities in this stage are represented by process tasks, so their details are described not in CMMN but in BPMN, and this is typical for complex case logic.

Shown below the normal *Active Case* functions are time-driven actions that manage case disposition. *Segmentation* is periodic reassessment of the client, possibly transferring to a different segment or closing the *Active Case*. The user event listener shows this may also be initiated manually, and it is always done upon receipt of the file item *Social care update* from *Intake*, regardless of its end state. *Delegation* is periodic reassignment of care team members to specific functions. The task *Close Active Case* is a process triggered either by *Segmentation* or manually by a case worker. Following closure, the stage *Active Case* remains *Active* for three months to handle outstanding invoices, after which it exits and moves to *Stored File*.

Stored File

The stage *Stored File* (Figure 46) is relatively simple. The case file information must be stored in a document management system with retention capability, including the ability to apply legal holds, if necessary. As needed, case workers may consult information in the stored file. After ten years in this stage, the case file information is archived and the stage may be *Completed*.

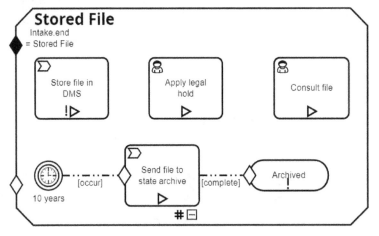

Figure 46. Child page expansion of stage *Stored File*

CHAPTER 7

Style Rules

In order to reveal the case logic as clearly as possible from the printed diagrams, we need to go beyond the requirements of the CMMN spec and define additional conventions. In Method and Style these may be formulated as *style rules*. In tools like Trisotech Case Modeler, models can be validated for conformance to the style rules automatically by the software.

In some cases, the style rules resolve ambiguities in the spec. In other cases, they require display of certain labels, symbols, or annotations allowed but not required by the spec, or require certain elements to match in parent- and child-level diagrams. And in still other cases they forbid certain diagram patterns.

A few of the style rules are specified as *warnings* rather than errors. Violations are not technically prohibited but allow the possibility of unwanted behavior, such as zombie states. Most of them, however, should be treated as *errors* and avoided whenever possible. In the figures below, the first diagram (overlaid with an X) illustrates the style error; the second diagram is correct.

Labeling

1. [0001] A task must be labeled (Figure 47).

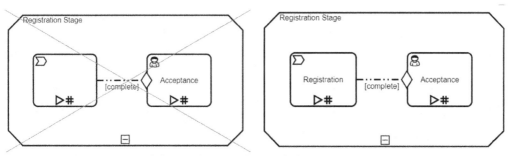

Figure 47. The process task is missing required label.

2. [0002] A stage must be labeled (Figure 48). It is easy to forget to label expanded stages.

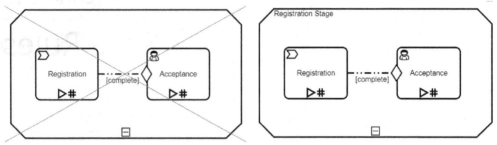

Figure 48. The stage is missing required label.

3. [0003] A timer event listener must be labeled with the timer expression (Figure 49).

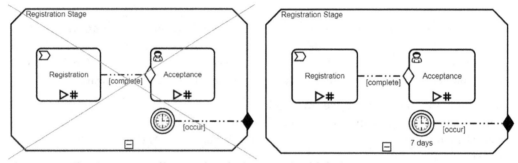

Figure 49. The timer event listener is missing required label.

4. [0004] A directional association to a timer event listener must be labeled with a standard event of the triggering item (Figure 50). This represents the trigger of the timer event listener. If no directional association is present, the trigger is activation of the containing stage.

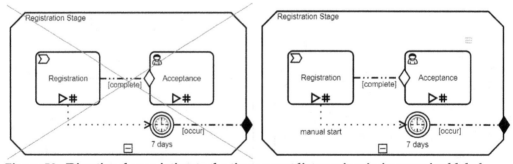

Figure 50. Directional association to the timer event listener is missing required label.

5. [0009] An ON-part link must be labeled (Figure 51). The label should be a standard event of the triggering item. It is not uncommon to see *complete* links unlabeled, but this is a style error.

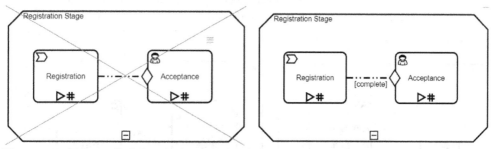

Figure 51. ON-part link is missing required label.

6. [0010] The names of tasks and stages must be unique (Figure 52). A task and a stage must not have the same name.

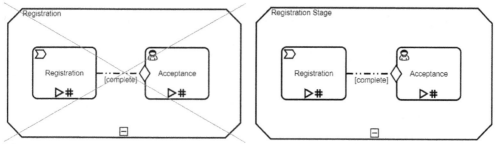

Figure 52. Task and stage must not have the same name.

Sentries

7. [0020] The source of an ON-part link must not be a sentry (Figure 53). There are diagrams in the spec that show links connecting two sentries, but this is an error. An ON-part link from a plan item must be drawn from the plan item boundary, not a sentry.[17]

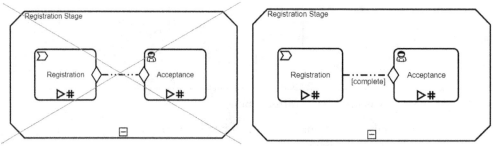

Figure 53. The source of an ON-part link must not be a sentry.

---

[17] Actually, this style rule conflicts with the CMMN spec when the trigger is *exit*. In that case, the spec says that a link drawn from the exit sentry of the triggering item to an entry or exit sentry of the triggered item is valid. It means the same as a normal *exit* link to the triggered item, and thus adds no new semantics. Also, the meaning of such a link drawn between two black sentries is ambiguous: which one is the source? For those reasons, this notation is not allowed by Method and Style.

8. [0100] ON-part links from a plan item should not cross a stage boundary (Figure 54, Figure 55). Violations of this rule are very often seen.

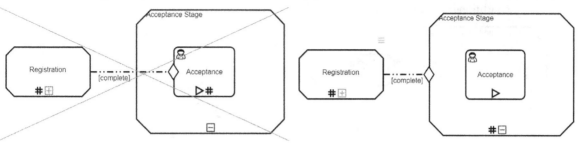

Figure 54. A triggered plan item must share the same containing stage as the triggering plan item.

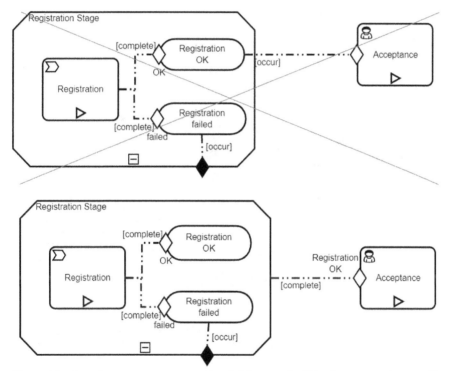

Figure 55. Another common example of this error is directly connecting a milestone to a plan item outside the containing stage. The milestone should be tested by an IF-part condition.

9. [0101] The label of an ON-part link from a plan item must be a standard event of the plan item (Figure 56). Do not label it with a condition, such as a milestone test. IF-part conditions should be visualized as sentry labels.

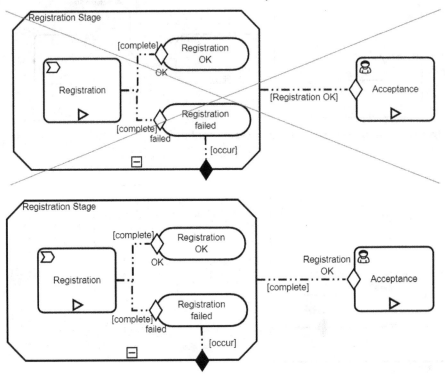

Figure 56. ON-part link label must be a standard event of the triggering item.

10. [0102] A sentry label represents its IF-part condition. When the condition tests a milestone of the preceding stage, the label should be a literal value matching the milestone name (Figure 57).

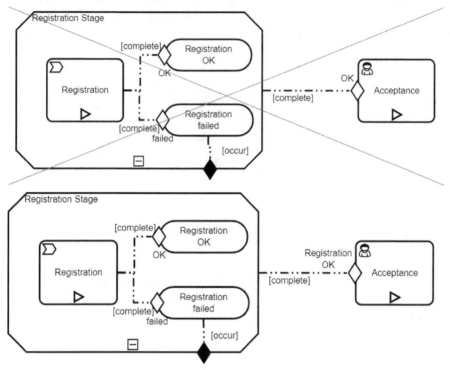

Figure 57. Sentry label does not match a milestone in the triggering stage.

11. [0112] The label of an ON-part link from a file item must be a file item standard event (Figure 58). For example, even though I wish *receive* were a file item standard event, it is not defined as such in the spec.

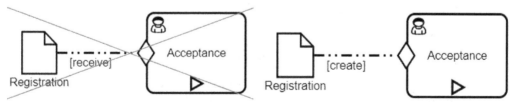

Figure 58. ON-part label is not a file item standard event.

Repeating Items

12. [0118] A *Repeatable* task or stage must either have an entry condition, be *Manually Activated*, or have a text annotation indicating a Repetition Rule (Figure 59). Otherwise a new instance of the plan item will always be *Active* and its containing stage will be unable to complete.

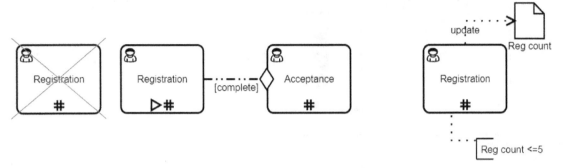

Figure 59. *Repeatable* **plan item must have either Manual Activation, entry condition, or Repetition Rule.**

13. [0119] Warning: If a *Repeatable* task or stage has no entry condition and is not *Manually Activated,* it should have a text annotation, representing the Repetition Rule, that references a file item updated by the task or stage (Figure 60).

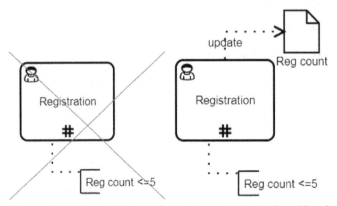

Figure 60. A Repetition Rule (text annotation) should reference a file item updated by the *Repeatable* **plan item.**

14. [0120] Warning: A plan item with an entry condition triggered by a *Repeatable* plan item and having no IF-part, should be *Repeatable*. Otherwise only the first instance of the triggering plan item trigger will be effective (Figure 61).

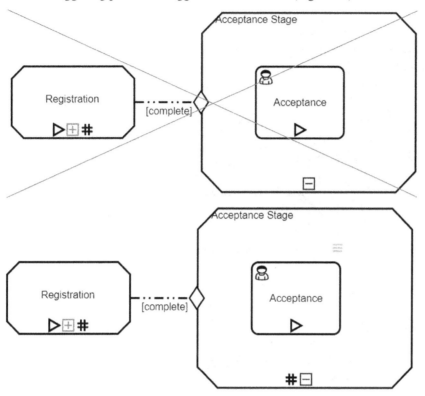

Figure 61. Plan item with repeating entry condition should be *Repeatable*.

15. [0121] A *Repeatable* plan item with a single entry condition (sentry) must be triggered by either a *Repeatable* plan item, a file item event, or a user event listener (Figure 62).

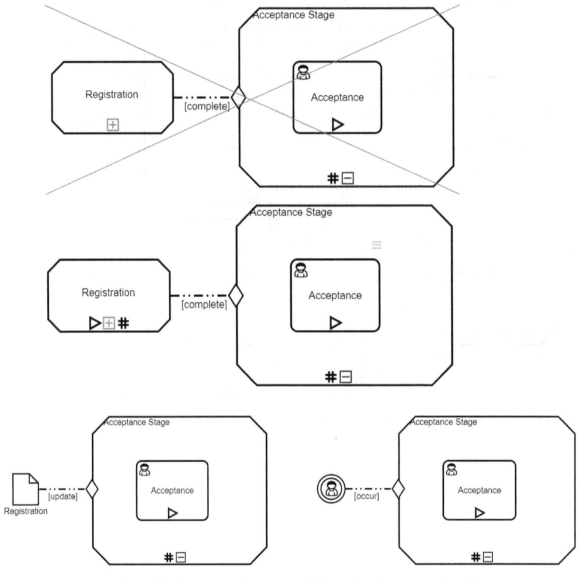

Figure 62. *Repeatable* plan item with entry condition must have repeating triggers.

Autocomplete

16. [0123] A stage marked *Autocomplete* must have at least one *Required* plan item (Figure 63). Otherwise the stage could *complete* automatically before any actions occur.

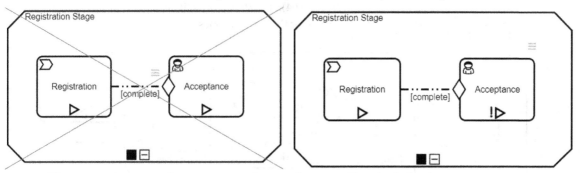

Figure 63. *Autocomplete* **stage must have at least one** *Required* **plan item**

Deadlocks (Zombie States)

17. [0105] Warning: If a stage has multiple milestones tested by the IF-parts of *complete* links, it should contain a single *Required* milestone triggered by all those milestones to ensure proper stage completion (Figure 64). In other words, it should be impossible to complete the stage without setting one of these milestones.

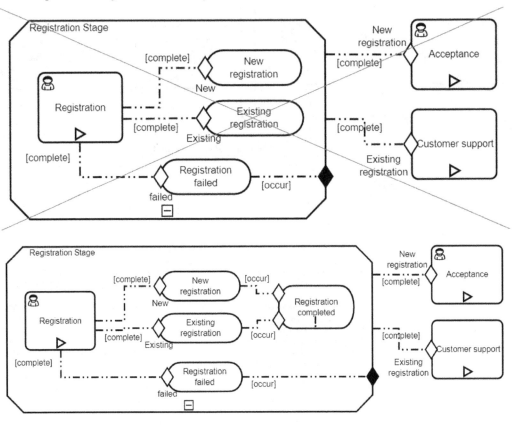

Figure 64. A stage with multiple non-exit milestones tested by complete links should have a single *Required* milestone to ensure proper stage completion.

18. [0125] A plan item with an *exit* event triggering another plan item must have an exit sentry (Figure 65).

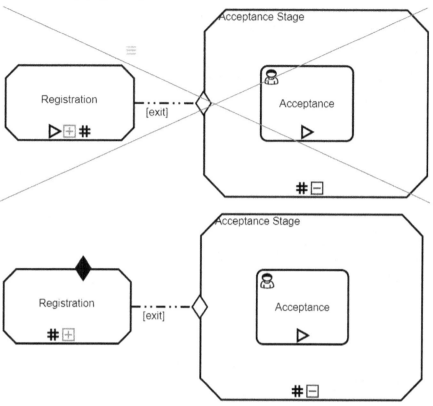

Figure 65. *Exit* **event missing corresponding exit condition (black sentry).**

CHAPTER 8

Declarative Modeling Patterns

In early drafts of the book, this chapter appeared toward the beginning, because I believed it would be easier for readers to grasp CMMN's declarative modeling patterns by showing them side by side with their BPMN equivalents. But some reviewers felt that this was unnecessary and interrupted the narrative flow. So with some misgivings I have placed it at the end, where it serves as a reference.

It's fair to say that just about any pattern that can be modeled in BPMN can be modeled in CMMN as well, and vice versa, although some work more naturally in one language than the other. And even though it means switching between models in two different languages, I strongly believe that fragments of case logic that are better modeled as BPMN processes should still be defined that way and incorporated into the case model as process tasks.

Since many readers are familiar with the Method and Style conventions for BPMN, in this chapter they are often used to describe the equivalent CMMN.

Sequence Flow

The most basic BPMN pattern is *sequence flow*. Task *b* starts when task *a* completes (Figure 66).

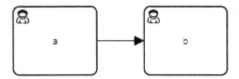

Figure 66. Sequence flow pattern in BPMN

Figure 67 is its CMMN equivalent. No IF-part label on the sentry means enablement of *b* is unconditional. In CMMN, this pattern applies to any plan item, not just a task.

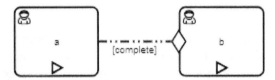

Figure 67. Sequence flow pattern in CMMN

Of course, in BPMN the process cannot complete until *b* is complete, but in CMMN, performance of task *b* is optional. Completion of task *a* just makes *b* *Enabled*, not *Active*.

Branch on End State

Figure 68 shows the BPMN *branch on end state* pattern. End state is a Method and Style concept that means how did the activity end? In BPMN Method and Style, the end states of task *a* are indicated by the labels on the XOR gateway immediately following the task. Thus BPMN Method and Style interprets Figure 68 to mean that the end state of task *a* is either "OK" or "Exception". If *a* completes in the state "OK", task *b* starts; if *a* completes in the state "Exception", task *c* starts.

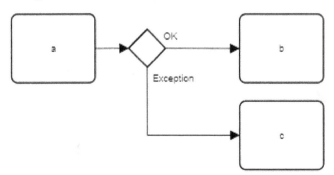

Figure 68. Branch on task end state pattern in BPMN

Figure 69 is the CMMN equivalent, making use of the CMMN Method and Style convention that the end states of a task are enumerated values of the implicit file item *[taskname].end*. Thus in Figure 69, task *b* is enabled if *a.end*="OK" and *c* is enabled if *a.end*="Exception". When the ON-part event is *complete* and the sentry label is a literal value, as is the case here, Method and Style interprets the sentry label as testing the end state value of the source plan item.

Branch on end state also applies to stages, where the end state is indicated by milestones.

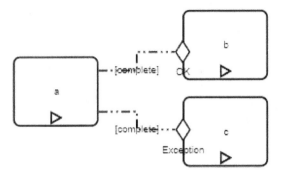

Figure 69. Branch on task end state pattern in CMMN

Parallel Split

In BPMN, the *parallel split pattern* (Figure 70) means when *a* completes, both *b* and *c* start concurrently, without condition.

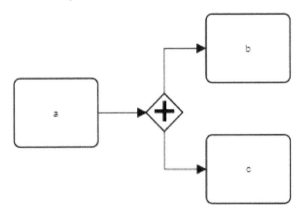

Figure 70. Parallel split pattern in BPMN

Figure 71 is the CMMN equivalent. The *complete* event of *a* is used to trigger both *b* and *c*. No IF-part label on the sentries means enablement is unconditional.

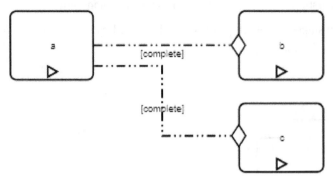

Figure 71. Parallel split pattern in CMMN

Conditional Split

In BPMN the OR gateway is used to indicate *conditionally parallel split*. Each gate has a condition suggested by the gate label. Unlike end states, which are exclusive, more than one gate may have a true condition, and all gates with a true condition are enabled in parallel. In BPMN Method and Style, OR gate labels do not signify end states, and may represent values of instance data that is not defined in the model. For example, in Figure 72, when *a* completes, *b* starts if that undefined variable has the value "critical" and *c* starts always, that is, unconditionally.

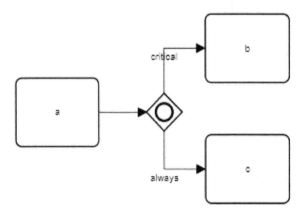

Figure 72. Conditionally parallel split in BPMN

In CMMN Method and Style, instance data affecting the case logic is visualized in the diagrams in the form of *file items*. In Figure 73, the Boolean file item *critical* is updated by *a*, as indicated by the directional association connector labeled "update". This notation is a Method and Style convention that says that task *a* updates the value of *critical*. The IF-part notation of *b* means when *a* completes, *b* becomes *Available* only if *critical* = true. Since *critical* is not an end state of *a*, we do not label the *b* sentry "critical" but use the full expression *critical* = true. [18] As in the previous example, *c* has no IF-part and is triggered unconditionally.

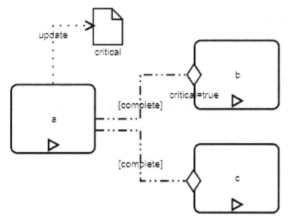

Figure 73. Conditionally parallel split in CMMN using file item IF-part

Alternatively (Figure 74), we could use the file item transition of *critical* ANDed with completion of *a* to trigger *b*. In that case there is no IF-part on the *b* sentry. When multiple ON-parts are ANDed (connected to the same sentry), the sentry waits for the last event before evaluating the IF-part.

The semantics of Figure 73 and Figure 74 are identical.

---

[18] Actually here, since *critical* is a Boolean, the sentry label could simply be "critical", but in general the full FEEL IF-part expression is used in the sentry label when not referring to the ON-part plan item.

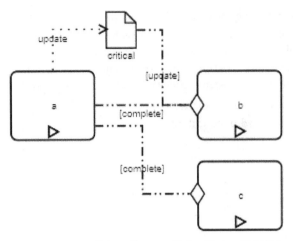

Figure 74. Conditionally parallel split in CMMN using file item event (ON-part)

Unconditional Merge

In BPMN (Figure 75), *d* starts after either *b* or *c* completes. This is only valid if *b* and *c* are alternatives, not parallel or conditionally parallel. Those result in *d* being triggered multiple times, called *multimerge* or an "unsafe model." Some modelers use an XOR gateway to merge the flows from *a* and *b*, but this means the same thing as no merge gateway at all, so I prefer the direct merge notation.

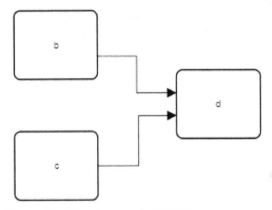

Figure 75. Direct merge in BPMN

In the CMMN equivalent (Figure 76), there is no need to worry about multimerge, since the sentry controls only the transition to *Enabled*. If *b* and *c* are parallel and *b* completes first, then completion of *c* has no effect since *d* is not *Repeatable* and has already transitioned to *Enabled*. If, however, *d* had a *Repeatable* marker, then completion of *c* would retrigger a second instance of *d*, behavior which is allowed in CMMN.

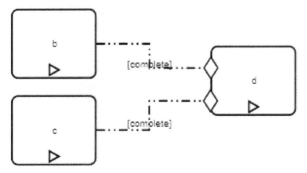

Figure 76. Direct merge in CMMN

AND-Join

Merging parallel or conditionally parallel paths in BPMN requires a *join*. If the paths are unconditionally parallel (Figure 77), an AND gateway join is required. An AND gateway join waits for all incoming sequence flows before continuing. Figure 78 illustrates an AND-join in CMMN. Here tasks *b* and *c* are unconditionally parallel, and the ON-parts of *d* AND the *complete* events of *b* and *c*, since they share the same sentry.

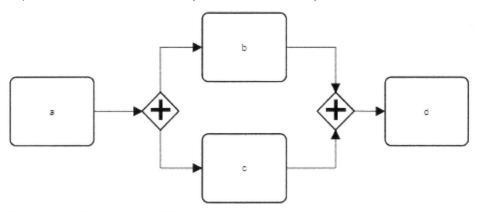

Figure 77. AND-join in BPMN

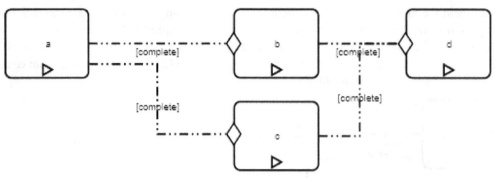

Figure 78. AND-join in CMMN

OR-join

Merging conditionally parallel paths in BPMN (Figure 79) requires an OR gateway join. An OR gateway join waits only for all incoming sequence flows that are enabled in the process instance, so in Figure 79 it waits for *b* only if *a* is "critical".

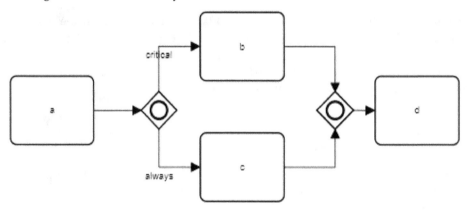

Figure 79. OR-join in BPMN

The OR-join equivalent in CMMN is trickier. We need to use the sentry IF-part to test the condition leading to the split. In Figure 80, if *critical* = true then *b* will be made *Available* and *d* will wait for completion of both *b* and *c* before triggering. If *critical* = false, then *b* is not triggered, and *d* will not wait for its completion. This could get really complicated if more than two paths are conditionally split.

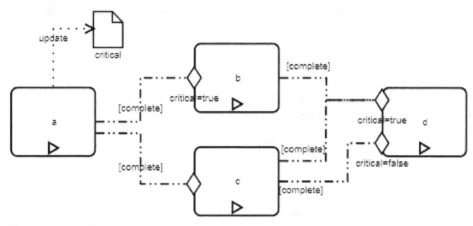

Figure 80. OR-join in CMMN

Start-Start

BPMN does not distinguish between when an activity is enabled to start and when work on it actually starts. It is assumed to start when the sequence flow arrives. For *Manually Activated* tasks, CMMN makes that distinction, which is quite useful in practice. In software like Microsoft Project, triggering task *b* on the *actual start* of task *a* is a common pattern. You can't do it in BPMN, but you can in CMMN. It simply uses the *manual start* transition, triggered by a case worker to move from the *Enabled* state to *Active*.

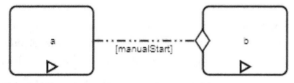

Figure 81. Start-start pattern in CMMN

Start-Finish and Finish-Finish

MS Project and similar Gantt chart-oriented tools allow you to say that task *b* must finish when task *a* finishes, or that task *b* must finish when task *a* starts. Again, you can't model these in BPMN but you can in CMMN.

In CMMN there are three ways a task or stage can "finish".

1.   It can *complete* from an *Active* state when its completion conditions, discussed in Chapter 4, are satisfied.

2.   It can *terminate* from an *Active* state upon case worker action.

3.   It can *exit* from any state when its exit condition, the black sentry, is triggered.

So to be more precise, the patterns shown below could be called *start-exit* and *finish-exit*.

Figure 82. Finish-exit pattern in CMMN

Figure 82 (left) says *b exits* when *a completes*. Figure 82 (right) says *b exits* when *a* either *completes*, *terminates*, or *exits*. The notation in the right diagram listing multiple standard events on one ON-part link is a visual shortcut; technically the spec asks for a separate sentry for each event. Trisotech uses this visual shortcut in their tool. Actually, *b* could finish earlier than *a* finishes, since *b* may *complete* before this *exit* transition occurs.

Similarly, Figure 83 says *b* finishes no later than when *a* starts. If *b* is not yet *Completed*, the start of *a* will automatically cause *b* to *exit*.

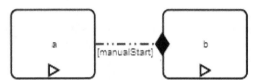

Figure 83. Start-finish pattern in CMMN

Start on Context Activation

The declarative modeling patterns described above were illustrated using tasks but they apply equally well to stages. In practice, the most common way a CMMN plan item becomes *Available* is none of those ways, but simply when its containing stage – called its *context* – becomes *Active*.

While a BPMN subprocess is considered an activity, in CMMN a stage is better thought of as a *state of the case*. More than one stage may be *Active* at the same time. In fact, since the case plan model as a whole is the top-level stage, this is true almost all of the time.

• A plan item becomes *Available* when its containing stage becomes *Active*. If it has no entry conditions, it immediately becomes either *Enabled* or *Active*, depending on whether or not it is *Manually Activated*.

• A plan item with one or more entry conditions becomes *Enabled* or *Active* when its containing stage is *Active* and one of its entry conditions is satisfied.

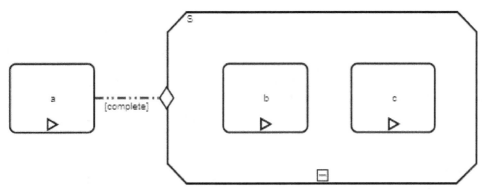

Figure 84. Start on context activation

In Figure 84, tasks *b* and *c* become *Enabled* when their containing stage *S* becomes *Active*. Because *S* is automatically activated – i.e., it has no *Manual Activation* marker – this occurs when *a* is *Completed*. If *S* had a *Manual Activation* marker, *b* and *c* would not become *Enabled* until *S* was manually started by a case worker.

What if we want to say *S* starts when *a* completes, and its contained task *b* becomes *Enabled* if *a* ends in end state "OK", and its contained task *c* becomes *Enabled* if *a* ends in "Exception"? Remember, ON-part links may not cross a stage boundary, so Figure 85 is INCORRECT..

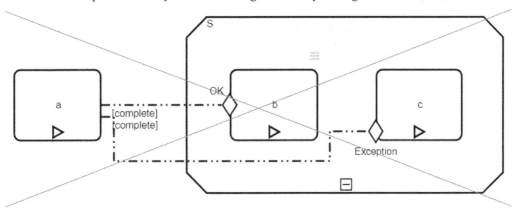

Figure 85. Triggering plan items across a stage boundary is an error

Instead, the *complete* event of *a* triggers the *start* of *S*, making *b* and *c* *Available*, awaiting satisfaction of their entry conditions. Now we cannot use the abbreviated IF-part labeling, since the sentry is not directly triggered by *a*'s *complete* event. Here the sentry label must be the full Boolean condition, like *a.end="OK"* (Figure 86). Note that these sentries have no ON-part link at all. This is perfectly fine. It means the IF-part is evaluated when the containing stage *S* becomes *Active*.

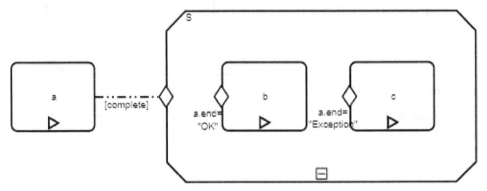

Figure 86. Trigger on end state outside the containing stage

Enable After Delay

The *timer event listener* can be used in a variety of ways add *lag* to the start of a plan item. The timer event listener has two properties, a *start trigger* and a *timer expression*, typically a duration. If the start trigger is omitted, by default the duration is measured from the moment the containing stage becomes *Active*. Otherwise, the start trigger is a standard event of a plan item or file item. The spec provides no visualization of the trigger, so in Method and Style, we indicate it with a directional association from the triggering item to the timer event listener, with the association label indicating the standard event. The label of the timer event listener is the timer expression. For example, in Figure 87, task *b* becomes *Enabled* one day after task *a* manually starts.

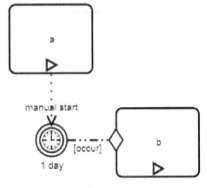

Figure 87. Enable after fixed delay

Enable No-Later-Than

We can combine a timer event listener with a user event listener to add *no later than* semantics. Figure 88 says *b* becomes *Enabled* no later than 1 day after *a* starts. The two entry triggers – user and timer events – are ORed.

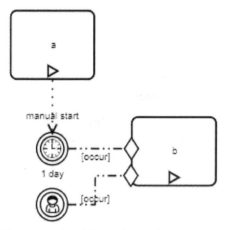

Figure 88. Enable *no-later-than...*

Enable No-Earlier-Than

In similar fashion, we can say *b* becomes *Enabled* no earlier than 1 day after *a* starts (Figure 89). Here the user and timer triggers are ANDed.

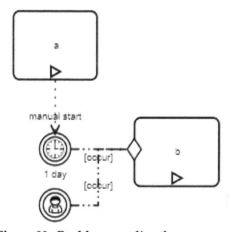

Figure 89. Enable *no-earlier-than...*

Finish No-Later-Than

In BPMN, finish-no-later-than is modeled with an interrupting timer boundary event (Figure 90).

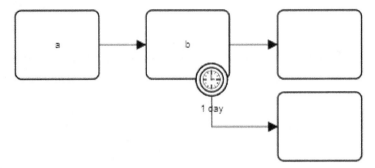

Figure 90. Equivalent BPMN *no-later-than* (interrupting timer event)

In CMMN we do this with an exit condition. Figure 91 says *b* is enabled when *a completes* and finishes no later than 1 day after *a completes*. If it is not complete by that time, the timer event will force *exit*.

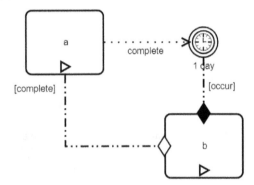

Figure 91. Finish *no-later-than*...

Event Gateway

In BPMN, an event gateway is commonly used to wait for either a message or a timeout, whichever comes first. Figure 92 says after sending a request, proceed to *b* if the response is received before the timeout, otherwise proceed to *c*.

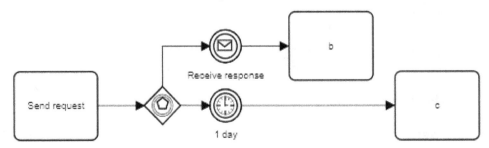

Figure 92. BPMN wait for response or timeout with event gateway

---

CMMN doesn't have the concept of a message, meaning data received from outside the case. For receiving a message, we make use of the file item *create* event. There are two ways to model this in CMMN, depending on whether receipt of the message is considered a human task or automated.

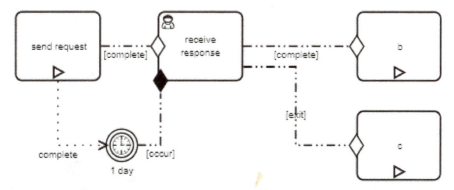

Figure 93. Wait for message (manual completion) or timeout in CMMN

In Figure 93 we model receiving the response as a human task, marked *complete* when the message is received. The timer trigger is specified as completion of sending the request; the duration is one day. If *receive response* is not complete when the timer event *occurs*, the timer forces *exit* of that task. In this case *receive response* has different events for *complete*, which proceeds to b, and *exit*, which proceeds to c.

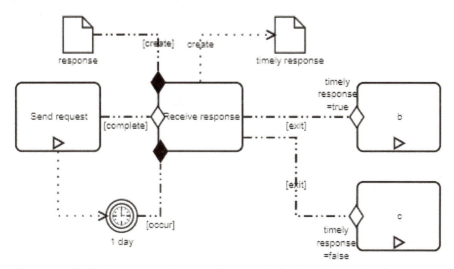

Figure 94. Wait for message (automatic completion) or timeout in CMMN

In Figure 94 receiving the response message is modeled as a file item *create* event. In that case, *Receive response* finishes only via *exit* after setting the Boolean end state file item *timely response*, which is used in the entry conditions of b and c.

Loop

In BPMN, a loop activity, indicated by a circular arrow marker (Figure 95), evaluates a data condition once it completes, and based on that either exits or performs the activity again. This cycle repeats until the "loop until" condition is satisfied. In Method and Style, we use a text annotation to indicate the loop condition. In Figure 95, the activity *Next* is performed once, after the loop exits.

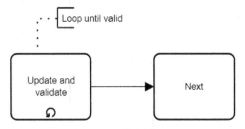

Figure 95. BPMN loop activity

In CMMN, we model a loop task or stage by making it *Repeatable* with two end states. It is enabled the first time with an initial entry condition and on subsequent iterations by testing the end state of the previous iteration in a Repetition Rule. In Figure 96 the end states of *update and validate* are "Errors" and "Valid". Here *update and validate.end* is tested both by the task's own Repetition Rule and the *complete* link to *Next*. When the implicit file item *update and validate.end* is "Errors", the Repetition Rule is true and a new instance of the task is enabled. Once an end state of "Valid" is achieved, *Next* is started and *update and validate* is no longer retriggered.

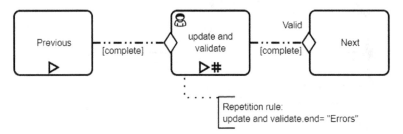

Figure 96. Loop in CMMN

Multi-Instance Sequential

In BPMN, a multi-instance sequential activity, marked with three horizontal bars, performs N instances of the activity, where N is the count of items in a process list variable. Sequential means the first instance must complete before the second one starts. For example, in Figure 97, the task is sequentially checking the inventory of each item of an order.

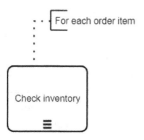

Figure 97. BPMN multi-instance sequential activity

In CMMN, the multi-instance task or stage must be *Repeatable* and increment a *counter* file item that is used in the Repetition Rule controlling iteration. In Figure 98, the task *Check inventory* is repeated for each item in a received order, modeled as file item *thisOrder*. The link from *Receive order* is triggered once, but on completion of each instance, the task is retriggered as long as the Repetition Rule,

```
counter <= count(thisOrder.item)
```

is satisfied. In Method and Style, the text annotation describing the Repetition Rule is required. The text annotation "for each thisOrder.item" is not necessary, but it may help to clarify the meaning.

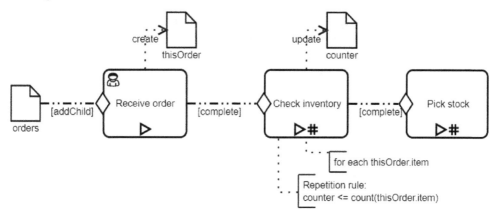

Figure 98. CMMN multi-instance sequential

As drawn in Figure 98, the follow-on task *Pick stock* is also triggered once per order item. If we wanted it to occur once instead, after all instances of *Check inventory* were *Completed*, we just need to change its sentry IF-part to:

```
counter = count(thisOrder.item)
```

Instances Overlapping in Time

CMMN can easily model a behavior that is more difficult in BPMN: multiple instances of a task or stage that are not strictly sequential or parallel but overlap in time. We've already seen it in *Pick stock* following a multi-instance sequential task (Figure 98). Multiple instances of *Pick stock* are enabled at different times, regardless of whether previous instances are still Active.

This can be done in BPMN, but it is clumsy and unfamiliar to most modelers. As shown in Figure 99, we can use a multi-instance sequential subprocess in which the task *Check inventory* is followed by a throwing signal event (or escalation event) that triggers a *non-interrupting event subprocess, Pick stock*. Each instance of the multi-instance subprocess thus creates a new instance of the event subprocess, and these instances may overlap in time. The process level containing the multi-instance subprocess and the event subprocess instances is not complete until all instances of these subprocesses are complete.

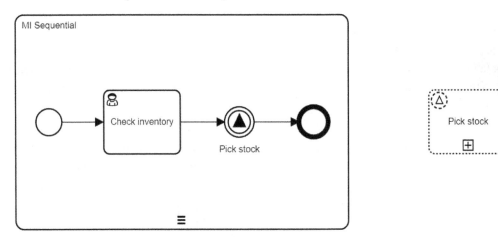

Figure 99. BPMN *Pick stock* **instances overlap in time**

Multi-Instance Parallel

In BPMN, a multi-instance parallel activity, marked with three vertical bars, performs N instances of the activity concurrently, where N is the count of items in a process list variable. Parallel means all N instances of the activity are started at the same time, and the activity is complete when all N instances are complete. For example, in Figure 100, the task is checking the inventory of each item of an order at the same time.

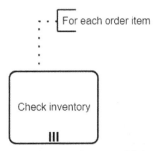

Figure 100. BPMN multi-instance parallel activity

In CMMN, the closest we can get to a multi-instance parallel task or stage is multi-instance sequential with instances overlapping in time triggered rapidly one after the other (Figure 101). In this case, we use a *Repeatable* short-running non-*Manually Activated* task (e.g., a script), *update counter*, which increments the file item *counter*. The Repetition Rule for this task is the same as in Figure 98, except now all N instances are created in rapid succession. Each instance of *update counter* triggers an instance of the *Repeatable* and also non-*Manually Activated* task *Check inventory*, which increments the file item *counter2*. Thus, all N instances of *Check inventory* start at nearly the same time, and the follow-on task *Pick stock* occurs just once after all instances of *Check inventory* are *Completed*, as required by its IF-part condition.

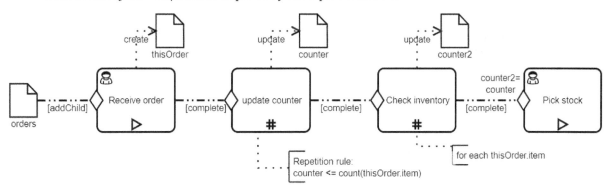

Figure 101. CMMN multi-instance parallel

Ad-Hoc Task Injection

One of the key features of most case management software prior to CMMN was the ability to add new tasks at runtime that were unanticipated at modeling time. In fact, this feature is central to the need to handle "unpredictable" case requirements. But CMMN lacks this essential element!

It's not hard to see why. Injection of ad-hoc tasks at runtime makes sense when the case is modeled in the user-driven style, but it is more difficult in ECA, when case behavior is driven by events and data conditions, since the file items controlling case behavior are defined at design-time.

Figure 102 illustrates one possible solution. Here the stage *Allow Ad-Hoc Tasks* is discretionary. That is not required, but it allows ad-hoc task injection to be restricted to certain users under specified conditions. Within that stage the task *Ad-hoc task* is triggered by a user event listener, which is by definition *Repeatable*. In the model, all instances of *Ad-hoc task* have the same name and basic template. It's not the most elegant, but it is consistent with the CMMN spec, and real CMMN-based software can clean up the rough edges in the runtime user interface.

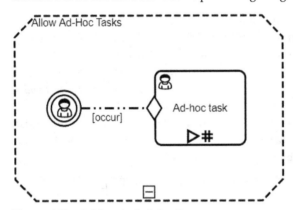

Figure 102. Ad-hoc task injection

CHAPTER 9

Executable CMMN with Method and Style

The concepts of Method and Style were originally designed for non-executable process models created by business users. With BPMN, those account for the vast majority, intended simply to capture the process logic for documentation, analysis, and improvement. Very rarely do most process modelers intend to automate the flows. The BPMN task force in OMG, however, was actually focused on making the diagrams executable on a process automation engine.

Making BPMN executable requires principally the definition of process *variables* and *executable expressions* used in gateways and a few other places. These are invariably provided by programmers, and visible only to users of the modeling tool. These variables and expressions make the process logic unambiguous to a programmer or an automation engine, but not to a stakeholder in the business, who has only the printed diagrams to go by.

BPMN Method and Style addresses this problem by using drawing and labeling conventions to *imply* the existence of certain process variables and gateway expressions without the modeler actually creating them. In particular, the concept of *activity end state*, discussed at length in Chapter 4 and elsewhere in this book, clarifies the branching logic and the relationship of parent and child process levels from the printed diagrams alone, without burdening the modeler with defining variables or executable expressions.

In my book *BPMN Method and Style*, I proposed that vendors of executable BPMN would do well by automatically creating the variables and gateway expressions implied by the non-executable models. It would not be hard to do, but almost a decade later, none of them have done it. That is understandable, since executable BPMN is typically created by programmers, and they may find little use for process variables created for them by business users.

More recently, DMN was introduced for decision modeling. Here the situation was a bit different, in that (a) decision models are normally intended for execution, not simply documentation; and (b) many business users want to define the actual decision logic – not simply "decision requirements" – themselves. The DMN standard was created with those differences in mind, and even created its own business-friendly expression language FEEL and standard tabular formats for executable logic. My book *DMN Method and Style* explains to business users how to do executable decision modeling themselves.

Now we have CMMN. I suspect that case modelers have a much greater interest in execution of their models than we had with BPMN, and at the same time a greater interest in directly specifying the case logic themselves. So it may be worth it, once again, to propose integrating Method and Style with model execution.

As before, it comes down to tool vendors automatically creating *real* case variables and executable logic – file items and IF-part expressions – from those *implied* by case milestones and sentry labels. The linkage between sentry labels and IF-part expressions, including the shorthand conventions, was explained in Chapter 4. Of course, modelers (and programmers) would be free to add their own variables and expressions, in any case. But executable case management implementations that accurately reflect the logic expressed in the CMMN diagrams would go a long way to fostering business-IT collaboration.

It requires a "smart" modeling tool and the will to engage business users in executable "low-code" design. Let's hope it happens!

Index

About the Author

Bruce Silver is Founder and Principal of methodandstyle.com and BPMessentials, the leading providers of training and certification in BPMN and DMN, the core standards of process and decision modeling. He is also Principal Consultant at Trisotech, a leading provider of business modeling and automation software. He was a member of the task force that developed the BPMN 2.0 specification in OMG and contributed to OMG's OCEB BPM certification exam. His book *BPMN Method and Style, 2nd Edition*, remains the standard reference on BPMN 2.0, and his more recent *BPMN Quick and Easy* teaches process modeling using Method and Style in a simple straightforward way.

He is also a member of the Decision Model and Notation (DMN) task force in OMG, and author of *DMN Method and Style 2nd edition* and the *DMN Cookbook*, the leading references on standards-based decision modeling. Together with Nathaniel Palmer of BPM.com, he co-chairs the annual bpmNEXT conference, a showcase of the next generation of business automation technology. His website methodandstyle.com provides news, commentary, and resources for practitioners of business process and decision modeling, and his company Bruce Silver Associates provides training and consulting in those disciplines.

Prior to founding Bruce Silver Associates in 1994, he was Vice President in charge of workflow and document management at the analyst firm BIS Strategic Decisions, which became Giga (now part of Forrester Research). He has Bachelor and PhD degrees in Physics from Princeton and MIT, and four US Patents in electronic imaging.

To contact the author, email bruce@brsilver.com.

www.ingramcontent.com/pod-product-compliance
Lightning Source LLC
Chambersburg PA
CBHW080427060326
40689CB00019B/4405